M000107113

The Magic of Healing

By the same author:

Little Book of Karma

The Magic of Healing

How to heal by combining yoga practices
with the latest spiritual techniques

Richard Lawrence

Thorsons

Thorsons
An Imprint of HarperCollins*Publishers*
77–85 Fulham Palace Road,
Hammersmith, London W6 8JB

The Thorsons website address is: www.thorsons.com

Published by Thorsons 2001

10 9 8 7 6 5 4 3 2 1

© Richard Lawrence 2001

Richard Lawrence asserts the moral right to
be identified as the author of this work

A catalogue record for this book
is available from the British Library

ISBN 0 00 711582 2

Printed and bound in Great Britain by
Martins The Printers Limited, Berwick upon Tweed

Illustrations by PCA

All rights reserved. No part of this publication may be
reproduced, stored in a retrieval system, or transmitted,
in any form or by any means, electronic, mechanical,
photocopying, recording or otherwise, without the prior
permission of the publishers.

Contents

Blessed are they who heal

List of Illustrations

Acknowledgements

I am indebted to the International Directors of The Aetherius Society who, as executors of Dr George King's published works, gave permission for the publication of those of his writings included in this book and, especially, the King Technique.

My deepest thanks go to Dr John Holder, Chairman of the Mind Body Spirit Festival and the Healing Arts Festival, for his superb Prologue; and to Brian Keneipp, international metaphysical author and magazine editor, for his enlightening Foreword.

I am also very grateful to Steve Gibson, Lesley Young, Liesel Butcher, Chrissie Blaze, Alyson Lawrence and Mervyn Smith for their input, and to Christopher Perry, Bryan Craig, Patricia Simmons and Nikki Perrott for assisting with research.

Prologue

We all live inside a miracle machine – our body is truly a wonder of creation and its exceptional ability to heal itself from disease is quite amazing. What we need to maintain good health is to give the body the tools it needs to do its job correctly. A balanced diet, plenty of water, deep breathing and a positive outlook on life will all help immensely. Healing is another tool, which is often overlooked.

It is the body that maintains harmony and cures disease, but all too often it is hindered in its task by questionable and often unproven modern medical treatments. The repression of disease by powerful drugs, with their inherent side-effects, is not the answer. Indeed, for many illnesses today two drugs are prescribed: one to 'cure' the illness and the other to combat the side-effects of the first drug. Often the 'cure' is worse than the illness. For these and other reasons, an ever-growing proportion of the population at large is turning to complementary or holistic therapies.

There are now more complementary therapists in the UK today than there are medical doctors. Healing, known also as spiritual healing, natural healing, psychic healing, pranic healing, etc., is being more and more widely used today. It is one of the most natural things in the world to do – a mother's natural instinct when her child hurts his leg, for example, is to rub it better. We all interchange energies on a daily basis, usually in an unconscious and instinctive manner. Healing is a way of transferring powerful natural forces to others in a conscious manner, and is an ability we all have inherent within us. It needs only to be practised to bring about quite remarkable results.

Healing adopts a holistic approach to illness and treats the body as an inter-related whole, not as a collection of unrelated parts. We have been provided with all the tools we need to cure disease, if only we look for them. Our ability to give healing to another is one of the most effective tools available to us today in the battle against disease.

I first met Richard Lawrence in 1971 at Hull University, when he was a young budding psychic. Richard has come a long way since then, and is now widely regarded as being one of the world's foremost experts on spiritual development and the paranormal. It has been my pleasure to have been one of his closest friends throughout his career and to have supported his efforts in bringing healing to the forefront of the public consciousness.

I am scientifically trained, with a PhD in Biochemistry, and have been an avid student of homoeopathy and other complementary medicines for over 30 years. I believe that healing is one of the safest, most effective treatments available today. We have all experienced, I am sure, what may be called a healing presence. When I was a young boy, my doctor would often cure me of my childhood illnesses by simply walking into the room. Disease is literally what it says – DIS-ease, or DIS-harmony or DIS-comfort. Healing brings ease, harmony and comfort, thereby nullifying the illness and restoring our natural balance.

In this excellent book, Richard describes a healing technique that is easy to understand, simple to learn, safe to administer, has no side-effects and is free, except for a bit of effort on the part of the healer and the patient. Most importantly it is a technique that works. I have personally tried it and know this to be true. I have met hundreds of people who have benefited from the healing technique described herein, and have never come across anyone who didn't feel better, in one way or another, from the treatment received.

But please do not take my word for it – try the technique yourself on your family and friends. I know that excellent results will be brought about and that your life will be enriched and expanded by doing so. All too often people turn to healing as a last resort when orthodox treatment has failed. Good health can and should be the norm – I believe it is our birthright. Use healing as a first resort and as an effective aid to both orthodox and complementary therapies.

It really does work like magic.

Dr John Holder, Chairman of the Mind Body Spirit Festival and the Healing Arts Festival

Foreword

Giving healing to others is probably the finest ability most of us can learn in these critical days on Earth. *The Magic of Healing* can get you from observer to healer in short order – and with a technique that can grow with you as you grow as a healer.

Spiritual Healing is a balanced, win-win activity.

The patient benefits through improved health; the healer benefits through learning to channel healing energies through him- or herself and experiencing the wonderful feeling of relieving some of the suffering of another.

The fact that science has yet to understand how such healing can work is why most people in the West think of such healing as magic. Richard Lawrence explains this 'mystery' in very simple terms.

Healing has a way of bringing us all back from the hard materialistic society in which we live, to a warmer and more comforting place within. Both the healer and patient start to sense the interconnectedness of all things during healing. It feels 'right' or natural to transfer some of the energies around us into the patient, in order to bring about a balance. Barriers caused by differences in religion, creed or social standing start to dissolve. The healing, which may have started out in order to heal a disease, begins to work on other aspects of both the patient and healer. The magical nature of the healing energy imbues and uplifts all it comes in contact with.

Yes, healing is indeed magical. In fact, healing is one of the cornerstones of magic itself. Magic can be defined as 'using supernatural power to influence natural forces.'

As you learn the technique contained within, you will start to use the supernatural power of the healing energies all around you to affect diseases caused by natural forces, such as viruses or bacteria. Learn to heal and you can start along the fascinating and rewarding path of a practising magician for the good of all. Through this path of mystical service to others you learn selflessness, the joy of helping others, the uplifting feeling of powerful energies coursing through you, and you start to feel the oneness of all things.

The technique Richard introduces, the *King Technique*, is the finest healing technique I know of. It is simple and very powerful. Like learning a simple yet well-balanced concentration technique, it is easy to learn and the benefits start immediately. Yet because it is a balanced technique, the more effort you put into this technique, the more you will get out of it – and the more you will be able to help others.

I had the privilege to spend many years working with the inventor of the *King Technique*, Dr King. He was able to heal with a glance. A few concentrated thoughts were all that were needed, if the conditions were right. Dr King spent most of his later years developing ways to help the world as a whole through very advanced mass healing techniques. Yet he never lost sight of the importance of personal healing.

You have in your hands a golden key to your future.

I recently met a man who first found the *King Technique* back in 1978. To him, it was the key he was waiting for. Within a few years, he told me, he was travelling the world giving healing to hundreds, from India to America. He experienced the ecstasy of several instantaneous healings, and opened many of his higher senses in the process. The *King Technique* changed his life and hundreds more. It opened his door to higher learning, ability and service to others.

You may not be in a position to throw yourself so deeply into healing, however this example serves to show that with the *King Technique* there are no limits. It will start to work the first time you use it, and it will grow in its effects the more you put into it.

I am very glad Richard has written this book. He brings together his understanding of metaphysics and psychic phenomena, his experience in spiritual healing and his gift for communicating difficult subjects in an interesting and understandable manner. His choice in offering to you, the reader, the *King Technique* was inspired. Richard presents the *King Technique* in a very clear and lucid manner. Within *The Magic of Healing*, Richard takes you into the reasons why this technique works and how you can maximize its effects within both you and the patient.

There is another aspect of Richard – something which is not focused on much, here in the West. I have known Richard for 25 years and he lives what he teaches. Richard lives and breathes service to others. He teaches various forms of spiritual development methods all over the world; he is the European Secretary of a non-profit organization, The Aetherius Society, dedicated to the peace and enlightenment of our world. He spends much of his time and energy for very little material remuneration. He could have used his considerable abilities for fame and material wealth, yet he has chosen instead to put his energies into helping and uplifting the world. This is the type of person to learn a healing technique from. The magic will be purer, and the results more balanced.

The Magic of Healing can be a turning point in your life – if you let it.

It is all here. The technique, the explanation behind the technique, and several enhancements to help you improve as a healer. The author is a proven channel for good and pure information (take this from me). All that remains is the most important point of all – your true effort and dedication to improve yourself, to heal those around you and the world.

It is an uncommon calling these days. I sincerely hope you will take up the gauntlet and join the ranks of the healers.

Brian Keneipp, Author of *Operation Earth Light – A Glimpse into the World of the Ascended Masters*; current editor of *Cosmic Voice* – a metaphysical journal first published in 1957; close disciple, friend and personal healer to Dr George King – inventor of the King Technique

1 *Energy Matters*

It's the time-old question: should we be ruled by the head or the heart? The answer to the question is, of course, by neither – or rather, both. There are times when we should listen more to the head, and others when the intimations of the heart should rule. Sometimes the intellect can make no sense of a feeling which subsequently proves correct; sometimes we get misled by emotionalism when intelligence or even basic common sense would have guided us far better. Healing definitely falls into the heart category, but the head has every reason to agree with it – as science, in its temple of rationality, is increasingly discovering.

Science and Metascience

I have no formal scientific training, so I can only look at the findings of those who have, and then draw parallels between them and a metaphysical view of the world. Of course there are many scientists who still balk at the very idea of anything remotely metaphysical. I bump into them frequently on radio and television shows when they are playing 'devil's advocate' against my paranormal beliefs – which, by the way, are absolutely normal nowadays according to all the latest polls. I remember such a scientist, whom you might describe as a jobbing sceptic, telling me on the train journey home after a somewhat acrimonious television show that he was having to wrestle strenuously with his conscience at the time. It turned out that he had just employed a nanny for his children and discovered to his dismay that – horror of horrors – she was a practising Christian. I had expected from the expression on his face for her to be at least possessed by evil spirits – but of course he would regard that as a delusional form of schizophrenia which should be medically treated. Was it morally acceptable, he wondered agitatedly, to leave the welfare of young, impressionable children in the hands of someone who held religious beliefs? How the tables have turned! A hundred and fifty years ago, the great theosophist and former humanist Annie Besant had her child taken away from her because her beliefs were regarded as dangerously anti-Christian. Dogma is, sadly enough, still alive and kicking, but now it infects science just as much as religion. Really, they should both be about the same thing: truth.

All Matter Is Imbued with Consciousness

I am glad to say, though, that there are some scientists who are discovering the validity of spiritual concepts through their work. Often shunned or ridiculed by their colleagues, they persevere with their groundbreaking discoveries. One of these is Gary Schwartz, Ph.D.,[1] who has devoted much of his time to proving that all things on the planet and beyond are energetic and alive. Working with Linda G. S. Russek,[2] he has used formal academic methods to develop the theory that all matter is imbued with consciousness, and that this consciousness lasts for ever. At a time when the old certainties of science have been well and truly thrown up in the air, this type of research is very refreshing and, in my view, absolutely essential.

Eager to protect his reputation, Schwartz kept his findings secret in the 1980s. This was partly because he knew it would damage his career if his work came out into the open: he would be dismissed by the orthodox academic community as a maverick eccentric and not taken seriously. But it was also because he was honest enough to recognize that he would be forced by his own conclusions to change his entire world view, which he did not want to do at the time. It was only after he met his collaborator, Russek, in 1993 that, emboldened by her uncompromising desire for the truth, he was willing to be open about his views.

The Perception of Love

As part of their research into living energy, Schwartz and Russek conducted an investigation into the perception of love and caring and its relationship to long-term health. They drew on a study into stress, which had been begun at Harvard University in the early 1950s, in which a group of men had been tested for their ability to withstand stress.

Russek did a follow-up on this group 42 years later, utilizing a theory called *energy cardiology*. This involves looking at the heart, or indeed any organ, not just as a material object, but as an energy-generating system which is perceiving and sending out subtle forms of energy. They used a method by which they could record brain-wave emissions and energetic emissions from the heart, both from Russek (the interviewer) and a number of interviewees. Through this method, an energetic correspondence was found between the interviewer's heart and the interviewee's head while they were together, even though they were not physically touching.

Schwartz and Russek specifically found that those men who had experienced a more loving childhood were more likely to register Russek's heart in their brain. The findings, published in 1994, indicate that there is a detectable transmission of energy between people who are in communication one with one another.

Schwartz and Russek's findings extend and confirm the work of neural researchers such as Eric Kandel, who wrote,

Even during simple social experiences as when two people speak to each other, the action of the neuronal machinery in one person's brain is capable of having a direct and long-lasting effect on the modifiable synaptic connections in the brain of the other.[3]

But, crucially, their research also showed that there can be some correlation between the head and heart at an energetic level, thus introducing the mysterious force of love into the equation.

Energetic Fields

Another of Schwartz and Russek's projects tested whether our bodies have energetic fields, and the ability of energy healers to tap into them. They found that, not only do these energetic fields exist, but that they are measurable. Their research revealed the following significant findings: that our bodies emit microwave signals which can be recorded on satellite dishes, and that the body emits high frequency x-rays. They also discovered that all physical objects, and biological tissue in particular, have an electrostatic charge. Through movement, this charge creates an electromagnetic field, which many of us would call an *aura*.

These results indicate much of what mystics have known for centuries. Druid and other so-called pagan teachings, for example, often regarded everything in the universe as a living part of the whole, which is continually evolving towards a more perfect state. Eastern philosophy is based on the belief that all matter in the universe is alive and is a part of the divine whole, which is another way of saying God. The Hindu term, *maya*, which appears frequently in the most ancient texts on Earth, the Vedas, signifies that all matter is a delusion which must be transcended.

A more new age view would be that matter exists at various frequencies of energy, which will be transmuted onto higher and higher levels as the cosmos as a whole evolves and ultimately returns to its divine source.

Living Memory

Schwartz and Russek's most controversial theory is the so-called *universal living memory hypothesis*, which concludes that everything has memory. This started as a result of an almost Damascene experience by Schwartz. In the early hours of a moonlit morning, he couldn't sleep as he pondered the wave-particle nature of light. He got out of bed and stood at the window looking out at the full moon sparkling on the bay before him. Then, like a flash – which he described as simultaneously physical, logical and intuitive – he realized that as the moonlight was reaching his window, his image was being reflected out into space. After one second, it would be transmitted approximately 186,000 miles into space. Minuscule as the intensity of that image would be, it would be carried as information-energy patterns spreading out into space. The memory of this event would exist forever as an image. Hence the concept of energy lasting, as memory, for eternity was developed. And eternity, as Woody Allen once succinctly put it, 'is very long, especially towards the end'!

Controversially, Schwartz contends that molecules, atoms and even the subatomic systems of photons and electrons which appear as waves or particles and are considered by most scientists to be inanimate, are not only animate, but learn and grow with experience. No wonder he was frightened for his reputation! What Schwartz really experienced in his scientific conceptualization was a sense of immortality, which others have felt before him. The American philosopher Ralph Waldo Emerson, when crossing a common one winter evening, described the sensation as follows, 'I became a transparent eyeball; I am nothing; I see all; the currents of the Universal Being circulate through me; I am part or particle of God.' Yeshe Tsogyel, the consort of Guru Padmasambhava who brought Buddhism to Tibet in the 8th century, said, 'When you finally discover me, the one naked Truth arisen from within, Absolute Awareness permeates the Universe.' The Indian mystic Gopi Krishna, who experienced the involuntary awakening of the inner spiritual force known as *kundalini*, wrote, 'This unimaginable Cosmic Intelligence is present at every spot in the Universe, and our whole personality – ego, mind, intellect and all – is but an infinitely small bubble blown on this boundless ocean.'

It is wonderful that one can quote from mystical sources from virtually every spiritual and philosophical tradition to describe parallel experiences which illustrate the oneness and timelessness of creation and the universe. Wonderful because it shows that the barriers between these different traditions are entirely manmade and artificial – the truth is universal and greater than them all. It is also wonderful that an increasing number of scientists are experiencing this same awareness of oneness and timelessness. It is particularly significant that such realizations should be perceived through the eyes of science in these days.

The Aquarian Age

Astrology tells us that we are now entering a new Aquarian Age, in which science and religion will merge. The exact date is disputed, but it is generally agreed that the latter part of the 20th century and the first decades of the 21st are a transition period between the Piscean Age, which started some 2,000 years ago, and the Age of Aquarius. It is not just a song from the musical *Hair*; it really exists!

The sign of Pisces is best represented by the expression of universal love (epitomized by Jesus, who came at the dawning of this Age); the sign of Aquarius is best represented by a metaphysical form of science – a science tempered by love. It is, in fact, the age of metascience.

Complementary Medicine

It is very much in keeping with this age that very practical conclusions are being drawn from science. Schwartz, for example, uses his universal living memory hypothesis to explain the success of certain forms of complementary medicine such as homoeopathy and aromatherapy. Homoeopathy was re-discovered by Samuel Hahnemann in the 18th century – I say re-discovered, because it is very likely that it was used in ancient Greece and possibly by other early civilizations. Though it has an impressive rate of success, it is still disputed by some scientists because they cannot see why it should work. As Sir Francis Bacon pointed out in his pioneering and often under-estimated work in the field of natural science in 17th-century Britain, science should look at events first and explain them afterwards, not the other way round.

Many scientists could still learn from Bacon in this respect. Hahnemann discovered that patients could be cured by administering minute quantities of the very substances which, in large quantities, caused the illness or problem they were suffering from. This remedy is diluted in water and then vigorously shaken, in a process called *succussion*, before being taken by the patient. The greater the dilution, the more potent the remedy is. Succussion works because it charges the remedy with natural energy, but why the dilution? Schwartz says it is because dilution potentizes the memory (consciousness) contained in the remedy by spreading it throughout the water, which is then 'charged' by succussion.

Aromatherapy, for its part, dilutes various flower oils to bring cures, usually applied through massage, but also invoking the sense of smell. Likewise, Schwartz believes it is the memory of the flower oil of, for example, a rose, which is most effective. The diluted water or carrier oil, he says, effectively stores the energy information connected with rose, which he calls 'the soul of the rose'.

The Collective Unconscious

Sometimes you have to be willing to be considered a bit mad to make serious progress in this world. It was, after all, during the period that the brilliant psychologist, Carl Jung had his so-called nervous breakdown that he developed the revolutionary concept of the collective unconscious. He also believed he was in communication with a number of discarnate entities during that period, though this was later explained away as a symptom of his mentally unbalanced state.

Whatever the truth of Jung's mental state at the time, it was then that he broke firmly with the Freudian school of thought which stated that all unconscious impulses, whether in our dreams or in waking states, come from within us and are usually caused by repression. Instead, Jung said that there is some kind of universal mind, which he called the collective unconscious, which we can draw upon. We might have a dream about something which means nothing specifically to us but is not just the result of some suppressed desire or fear within us, as Freud might have concluded. Instead, it could be something we have picked from the sea of consciousness around us, which has a universal meaning. Among other things, this goes a long way towards explaining the increasingly common phenomenon of the accurate precognitive dream, which cannot be satisfactorily explained in terms of the subconscious mind. How could the subconscious have a premonition about the future if it is composed of repressed memory?

The Akashic Records

Jung was tapping into something which had been referred to thousands of years earlier in Sanskrit writings as *akasha*. The father of Raja Yoga, which is the yoga of oneness with the divine through mental and psychic control, is generally recognized to be Sri Patanjali. He was a truly enlightened master shrouded in mystery, though we know he lived in

India several centuries before the birth of Jesus. He taught his students how they could know everything that has happened in the total history of the planet by reading what are known as 'the akashic records'. These are fields of thought energy, in which all the thoughts and events of history are inscribed. Using a rarely attained, deeply meditative trance condition known as *samadhi*, these records can be revealed in their entirety to the meditator.

Patanjali's aphorisms teach serious students to break down the barriers of mental limitation through advanced meditative practices which enable them not just to tap into their own higher consciousness, but also the sea of consciousness around them. *Akasha*, literally translated, means 'the ethers of space' – that in which all matter, thought and energy are contained.

Good Vibrations

The only thing which differentiates the various manifestations of energy in the ethers is the *frequency* at which they vibrate. All life is energy in one state of etheric vibration or another, so everything is a result of vibration. Even on the purely physical level, Nikola Tesla, derided in his day as 'the mad inventor', discovered among many other things the principle of mechanical resonance, which shows that the introduction of a specific and often gentle physical vibration which is in tune with a particular object can have devastating effects upon it, and ultimately cause it to disintegrate. On the cosmological level, it is believed that microscopic vibrations, imprinted when our universe was smaller than a golfball, have inflated and now stretch across the universe, constituting the ripples that develop into galaxies and clusters of galaxies. On a mental level, thoughts and feelings travel as vibrations or waves. When they are picked up by the mind of another, we often call the ability 'psychic', but it should really be considered a perfectly normal expression of human potential.

Just as scientific disciplines such as psychology, neurology and medicine are starting to discover akasha, so is physics. Now that we know that there is far more invisible matter than visible matter in the universe (possibly 10 times as much), it is difficult for astrophysicists and cosmologists, try as they might, to avoid metaphysical questions.

Time Travel

Today's physicists realize that there must be major conglomerations of undetected mass, or galaxies would literally fall apart, because there is not enough detected mass to exert sufficient gravity to hold them together. Black holes, where dark or invisible matter exists and where the mass is compressed into such small areas of extraordinary density that intense gravitational pressures are exerted, raise yet more issues. For one thing, they distort time, which slows down in the vicinity of a black hole. This is because space is so warped that light moves in circles and time can virtually stand still. After all, time only exists relative to the movement of planetary bodies. Our measurement of the 24-hour day, for example, is based upon one revolution of the Earth. If that speed was altered by fluctuations in gravity and mass (which, incidentally, some believe it already has been to a small degree), then the length of time of that 24 hours alters.

Prominent scientists such as Stephen Hawking, who at one time dismissed the concept of time travel out of hand, now accept it. It has moved out of the realms of science fiction and is being pondered as definite scientific fact. Just as Dickens' portrayal of the injustices of capitalism was reflected a hundred years later in the general acceptance of the need for a welfare state, so some of the concepts of science fiction are now being considered to be serious candidates for scientific enquiry. It is even believed that some of the apparently 'impossible technology' of *Star Trek* will actually happen one day – and is probably already happening somewhere in space. Even the one-time sacrosanct idea that the speed of light is the ultimate velocity is no longer taken as gospel. In short, much as happened to traditional religion, the former certainties of science are being assailed by doubt. The Holy Grail of those pivotal figures who virtually invented and gave us what we know as physics, such as Newton and Einstein, is now under the microscope.

Higher Dimensions

One of the main focuses of the current scientific debate concerns dimensions. The three physical dimensions of length, breadth and height, with time generally accepted as the fourth, are no longer sufficient to explain modern cosmology. Hence the development of ideas like 'superstring theory', which suggests there could be six or more dimensions in creation. Add to this the serious examination of so-called virtual universes, which we cannot detect because they exist in some other dimension, where different parts of creation are perceived as co-existing and overlapping one with another, and it is utterly impossible to keep physics out of the realms of metaphysics, or science out of the realms of metascience.

This fusion of different approaches, whether from the head or the heart, is to be welcomed. But there is something, I believe, which is more important than either. It has had a very poor press in orthodox science to date, but is gaining in validity as the former intellectual certainties are becoming patently uncertain, and objective reality is hard to find and often impossible to prove. I refer to subjective, firsthand, personal experience.

Personal Experience

In 1999, a report in the *British Medical Journal* revealed that a research programme at Southampton University, which had set out to investigate the effectiveness of antibiotics, unintentionally came up with a very unexpected finding. The most relevant factor in patients' recovery from a sore throat had nothing to do with antibiotics at all – it was whether the doctor chatted to them and listened to their concerns. Could one of the reasons for this be the transference of subtle energies during the conversation, which Schwartz and Russek and others had proved scientifically do exist? The concern of the doctor in the well-being of patients could have generated a natural interchange of energy between them, which had a direct bearing on recovery. The so-called 'bedside manner' could be more than an idea – it could have a direct and tangible healing effect.

I don't think you need any proof of this. You know from your own personal experience that there are some people who just make you feel better. They are not necessarily your closest family or friends – they may just be acquaintances you bump into at work or on social occasions, but when they are in a room you immediately feel uplifted, calm or some other tangible feeling. This is a simple transference of their natural energy to you. You might be standing on the other side of a packed room and you just know a certain person has come in without even seeing them. You have literally picked up their vibes.

Even if this has never happened to you, you can bet it has to your pets, if you have them. How do they know that their owner is coming home at an unexpectedly early time when they are waiting at the door for them to arrive? Animal instinct, you might say – but how does that operate? Again, by a transference of energy from you, through the ethers of space, to them.

How do you know that a building has been a happy or sad place by just walking into it? Because the vibrations are implanted in the walls by the people who have lived there before. Cutting-edge scientists might call it the universal living memory hypothesis, ancient Hindu philosophers akasha, but to you or me it is just plain personal experience.

I am a great believer in the value of subjective experience. One of the workshops I regularly run, *Unlock Your Psychic Powers*, is based on the fact that everyone who attends is guaranteed to have a personal psychic experience to their own satisfaction or their money back. This may sound like a gimmick, but to me it is a matter of principle. I want those who come to the workshop to realize from personal experience, in one way or another, that they are psychic. Others may disbelieve them, but they must know, and if they don't the workshop has not been successful. So far I have a better than 99 per cent success rate, from the hundreds of students who have taken the workshop. This percentage, I think you will agree, is enough to be regarded as proof – especially since, financially, they have an incentive to fail!

Here are three tests you can use to discover from personal experience whether you have the ability to detect energy in the ethers around you.

Three Energy Tests

Energy Test One

The next time you get a letter and you don't know whom it's from, don't open the envelope. Hold it between the fingers of both hands and see what energies you detect. Do any thoughts pop into your head, apparently from nowhere? Do you feel any particular mood such as happiness, sadness, excitement, fatigue? Do any images come into your head which you have no reason to think about at the time? Write down on a bit of paper anything that comes to you, no matter how apparently absurd. Then open the letter and see if there is anything in it which relates to what you've jotted down and can be considered beyond the scope of reasonable coincidence. If so, you have tapped into the mind energies in the letter before you opened the envelope.

Energy Test Two

The next time you visit a place for the first time, especially a building, spend some time tuning in to the atmosphere and see what thoughts, feelings and images come to you. Again, the less you know about the place beforehand, the better. If you are aware of its history, that may influence your thinking and cause you to invent or imagine things which are not really the energies you are picking up. Become the observer and just see what comes to you, no matter how remote it may appear at the time. See if any of your impressions turns out to be accurate. If you get good at this, try doing it just *before* you arrive somewhere new – which is more difficult because you have to tune in and pick up the vibes over a distance.

Energy Test Three

The next time you are about to meet someone for the first time, spend some time with your eyes closed, allowing their energies to connect with you. The less you know about them, the better. Just think their name or whatever information you have been given and then allow whatever feelings, thoughts or images are in the ethers around them to travel to you. Then, when you meet them, see if anything you picked up beforehand was accurate. It is always best to write your impressions down before meeting them, so that you have something in black and white that tells you it's not just a case of your imagination or your memory playing tricks on you. You really did pick up these things which turned out to be accurate.

These three tests will work only if you really try them with an open mind. They may not work first time, because of the way your mind is conditioned to operate. This is a different pattern of mental activity – you are being receptive, rather than proactive – and that is easier for some people than others to access. If you find it difficult, be patient with yourself and gradually coax yourself into the right receptive state of mind.

It may be, of course, that you have already had an experience like this and need no further proof. Still, do these exercises, because, as well as giving you some tests, I have surreptitiously introduced a lesson in healing. When you give healing to a patient, this ability to tune in to them and their surroundings will help immensely. As well as acting as tests for the existence of subtle energies in the ethers around us, they are techniques for developing your psychic awareness.

This is not something you just do at specific times when you are actually practising healing. You can do it whenever you choose, constantly enhancing your psychic awareness in all situations. This will also make you far better prepared for life in general. Your results will become more and more reliable the more you practise, and you will learn to tell the difference between a genuine psychic impression and your imagination. All too often we do not have all the information we need in a given situation. This ability will help you to become more understanding and aware when dealing with other people. It is also an ability which proves beyond all doubt that there is a dimension of existence beyond space, time or even the movement of planetary and other bodies – and that is mind.

States of Mind

It is not difficult to see that mind is a higher dimension than time, because we know that an hour can take a long or a short time depending on what we are thinking or feeling at the time. Then there is the incredible 'coincidence' of creation, which could so easily have gone (in theory at least) in an entirely different direction. There must have been a cosmic brain behind creation for it to be so perfectly balanced. As the great Chinese mystic Lao-Tzu says in the *Tao Te Ching*:

There is a thing inherent and natural
which existed before heaven and earth.
Motionless and fathomless.
It stands alone and never changes;
It pervades everywhere and never becomes exhausted.
It may be regarded as the Mother of the Universe.

But consciousness, which is not yet fully understood by any neurologist, is not limited to the brain. In 2000, two scientists working at Southampton General Hospital (Southampton must be a good location for metascience!) discovered that consciousness continues even when a patient is brain dead. These two doctors, Parnia and Fenwick,[4] interviewed 63 heart attack sufferers who had technically died and then been resuscitated, about their period of unconsciousness. They discovered that seven of them had experienced consciousness even while their brains were no longer functional. They had had what are often called 'near-death experiences', which are taken as evidence of life after death and the existence of the soul.

This finding also demonstrates that it is possible to tap into mind without using the physical brain. Dr Parnia concluded that the brain is an intermediary, rather than a source, for mind – just as a television acts as an intermediary, turning waves in the air into a picture or a sound.

I realized something strange was going on when I was a teenager and had the ability to find people. I didn't think of it as in any way psychic – it seemed perfectly natural at the time. If I needed a lift to town, I would often wait until I felt the time was right, then walk out of the house and, sure enough, someone would drive by who knew me and give me a lift. If I needed to find someone, providing I was in the right mood I could often do so, even though the person might not be in a place they would normally be. Nothing spectacular about this, just a useful, time-saving ability. If you think about it, in your own childhood you probably experienced something of a psychic nature which seemed perfectly natural at the time.

I realize now I was tuning in to the flow of mind waves in the ethers. But, I also knew, even then, that how I felt at the time was important. I saw it as a certain mood, which is another way of saying 'state of consciousness'. Psychic ability is much more about feeling than it is about thinking.

Consciousness

The word 'consciousness' derives from the Latin words *scire* ('to know') and *cum* ('with'). It literally means 'to know with'.

Some interesting experiments into how consciousness works were carried out by Benjamin Libet and Bertram Feinstein[5] and their colleagues in the 1970s, which involved analysing brain surgery patients who were awake during surgery. Libet and Feinstein discovered that it took one-hundredth of a second for a touch stimulus on a patient's skin to travel as an electrical activity along the neuronal pathway and reach the brain, but it took about half a second for patients to verbally report the stimulus. They could respond behaviourally by, say, pushing a button in less than a tenth of a second. This proved that a self-aware consciousness (sufficient to make a verbal response) is slower than an instinctive, behavioural response by almost half a second. In other words, the two are separate processes.

Even though these are minute fractions of time, I believe this confirms the findings of yoga meditation: that there are seeds of consciousness within the mind that can be eliminated by meditation to achieve a purer, more direct state of awareness. This process was described in Raja Yoga as 'frying the seeds'.

Psychic awareness is part of this process of using one's initial instinctive responses to tune in to a situation. The intellect can be a hindrance to this, which is why sometimes academically trained people find it more difficult to be intuitive. Their conditioned analytical response can obstruct an instinctive response to life. They sometimes need to re-train themselves in order to listen to their inner voice.

The creative process, too, is instinctive rather than intellectual, described by Tchaikovsky as coming suddenly and unexpectedly like a root shooting up through the earth at great speed and instantly sprouting forth branches, leaves and blossoms. The Impressionist painters were criticized by the art establishment of the day for painting their works too quickly – and yet their works have dwarfed those of slower artists who were championed by the very people who criticized the Impressionists.

This type of consciousness is also the key to why dreams can be so important. The Siberian chemist Mendeleeff dreamed of what we now call the periodic table of elements, which is still in use today. Paul McCartney says that the music for his most performed song, *Yesterday*, came to him in a dream. These examples illustrate that consciousness is not restricted to the deductive process or even what we might consider to be self-awareness. In dreams, when the conscious part of the brain is negated, other aspects can be contacted. Psychologists refer to these aspects the *unconscious*. Mental relaxation can also lead to contact with higher, inspirational aspects of mind. Wagner was relaxing by the River Rhine listening to the ceaseless modulations of the river when the opening bars of *Das Rheingold* were born. And Heisenberg was on vacation walking and swimming when he gained the basic insights into quantum mechanics which were to have such an awesome effect on scientific progress.

Aspects of Mind

Psychology has explored one aspect of the unconscious mind – the *subconscious* – but barely touched on the other, even more important one – the *superconscious*. This is the aspect of mind which includes everything from psychic awareness to the deepest mystical states in which spiritual figures from all traditions experienced a oneness with the divine and were able to merge their identity into it.

This is not just true of mystics in the East, but also includes those from Christian, Jewish and Islamic traditions, who identified themselves with a divine being. The 15th-century Christian mystic Catherine Adorna of Genoa, for example, said, 'My being is God, not by simple participation, but by a true transformation of my being.' The 14th-century Kabbalist Moses de Leon wrote, 'God, in his supreme manifestation, where the fullness of His Being finds its final expression in the last and all-embracing of his attributes, is called I.' And the 12th-century Sufi mystic Ibn al-Arabi said, 'If thou know thine own existence thus, then thou knowest God; and if not, then not.' These are all further illustrations of the fact that perception is not so much a product of the religious or philosophical tradition from which a person comes, but how much he or she is manifesting inner potential.

I am often asked whether psychic development is a correct use of one's spiritual potential. Some teachings, particularly from the East, stress the importance of detaching from these powers and focusing within, in order to gain contact with the higher self. Is psychic development an obstruction to spiritual development? The answer is most definitely no, with one proviso: that you use your psychic abilities to help others. If you do this, you will enhance your own development along the way. And when you ultimately come to the stage when you choose to go beyond the psychic arena into deeper mystical states, you will be able to do so.

Those who teach otherwise are missing out on a major point, namely that these abilities are meant to be used to help others, which is the very essence of the new age spirit. It is completely valid to develop psychically, not just for the sake of your own development but also to help other people and express your own inner potential more fully. And there is no finer way to do it than healing.

Summary

We live in a sea of energy, manifesting in many different ways and on many levels or dimensions of existence. An extension of the light spectrum leads to the invisible light spectrum. If this were extended indefinitely, what type of matter would exist there? Would the material light photons gradually become spiritual photons? Now that speeds faster than light are seriously accepted, along with concepts like fluctuating time curves and multi-dimensional existence, it is possible to embrace the psychic world as something concrete (if that isn't a contradiction in terms), rather than ethereal.

Traditionally, mystics have avoided scientific explanations for their beliefs. They knew from their own experiences and meditations that the psychic world existed, but regarded it as something separate and unrelated to the physical world. They talked of higher spheres, which were unrelated to and disconnected from material existence. Now it is possible to see these higher spheres as a continuation of rather than an alternative to physical existence.

Frequency and Vibration

It is all a matter of frequency and vibration. Once you accept that mind exists as energy in a sea of vibrations, then you can accept mind waves just as readily as radio waves, light waves or sound waves. At a different frequency of mind, you could have other types of material existence. On a higher sphere you could indeed have angels with harps and wings – though they are far more likely to be actively engaged in humanitarian work, manifesting mind energy in a certain form. In the same space on another much lower frequency level you might have what we regard as the physical world – it could be the city of Tokyo or the Sahara Desert. The etheric energy which contains all these multi-dimensional planes manifests at different energy levels depending on the frequency of mind which exists there. This type of new age concept gives a far more complete understanding of the psychic world than the old-fashioned ideas, which completely separated the material from the spiritual. Einstein could not have realized just how accurate he was when he said, 'Our separation from each other is an optical illusion of consciousness.'

I remember a radio interview with another scientific 'devil's advocate', who asked me to prove all my assertions about psychic and spiritual experience there and then. Eventually I asked him whether he loved his wife. (Not that I had any reason to doubt it, by the way!) I knew that on national radio he would in any case say 'Yes'. I then asked him to prove it there and then, which of course he couldn't. He had to admit that the heart can be a more valid guide for living than the head. Whatever their heads might think, people who listen to their feelings know that there is something to all this psychic stuff.

2 *Psychic Sense*

The most magical aspects of healing work on a psychic level, later reflecting on the physical body. As illustrated in the previous chapter, scientists are discovering that we inhabit a universe which exists on many psychic and mental levels simultaneously. As with the macrocosm, so with the microcosm: the individual patient has to be healed at every level, especially the psychic, because this is so neglected by most other medical systems.

There are many dubious psychic claims out there, which lead some people to (wrongly) dismiss the whole concept. This type of negativity can be even more dangerous than deluded psychism, because it can condemn genuine psychics as mentally unstable. The patronizing disdain which has surrounded William Blake's obvious clairvoyance, during his own lifetime and since, is just one famous example. How many unknown cases are there of inexperienced psychics being classified as schizophrenic? And conversely, how many mentally unstable people have been believed to be psychics? This is a field which cries out for serious study. In fact I have recently been contacted by a major hospital in London that is looking into just this.

For most of us there is no need for either of these extremes. Balanced psychic development is completely safe and totally liberating. Awakening one's latent faculty of ESP in a controlled way can be sheer excitement and revelation, and no vehicle for psychic development is better than the magic of healing.

The starting point is to realize that you are psychic. Don't brush your own psychic experiences under the carpet for fear of ridicule or 'losing the plot'. We are all psychic – the secret is learning to recognize it. Why not test it for yourself with this simple psychic review?

The Psychic Review

Relationships

Look back over the relationships which have really meant something to you, and possibly still do, and go through them one at a time. How did you first meet? Did you follow any kind of gut feeling which led to the conditions under which you met? Were you prompted to go to a particular place at a certain time, and if you hadn't would you ever have met? Did you instinctively know what made the other person tick before you got to know them? Was there some kind of 'déjà vu' about it? Did you develop a relationship which led to you knowing what they would say before they opened their mouth? Were some of these instances just too accurate to be a coincidence?

Were there occasions when you were separated by distance but you still knew what was on their mind or what they were doing, even though you had nothing rational to go on? Did you sometimes know where they were even though they had never told you? Were any of these instances too much to be a coincidence? Did they go beyond what you could deduce from your knowledge of their personality – especially in the early stages, when you did not know them well? Just co-incidence ...?

Work

Did you ever get a feeling about a job which on the face of it wasn't so good – less money and opportunity – but you knew it was right for you? Did it turn out to lead to some unexpected success? Have you followed a lead which logic said was not promising and yet something within you said, 'stay with it' and you got an unpredictably good result? Have you ever known that a client or colleague was not reliable instinctively, even though you had nothing to go on, but you turned out to be right? Just haphazard ...?

Holidays

Have you been somewhere and recognized it even though you had never been there before? Did you get a premonition in a dream which told you not to take a particular flight or other journey, which would have led to disaster or delay if you had not listened to your inner voice? Have you ever ignored the tempting pictures in a brochure and followed your gut instinct instead to go somewhere else, and when you got there found your feelings to be more reliable than the information supplied by the travel company? Was it uncanny how you knew things about your holiday before you got there ...?

Health

Do you ever know what's good for you – the right foods to eat, the exercise you need, what treatments will work for you even though this is not exactly what you have been recommended by experts? And did these things really prove to work for you? Have you ever felt a pain for no apparent reason and then found the person you were sitting next to had a pain in the exact area you felt it, as though it were a sympathetic reaction?

Have you ever got the feeling or impression to phone or visit someone who was not expecting you, to find that they needed your help exactly then because of an illness or accident? Have you ever got a feeling you should avoid a particular meal or party and later found that others who went became ill through the food or contagious illnesses going around?

Have you ever known that you were or were not ill despite all advice to the contrary? How about others – do you sometimes know what's wrong with them without being told? Could all this be explained away as just a fluke, or is there a pattern here ...?

Spirituality

Is there a particular type of mysticism or spirituality that you instinctively understand, although you have never been trained in it? It might be Taoism, Hermetic magic, feng shui, yoga or something else that you were never taught at home or school? Do you ever feel a warm peace inside when you stop thinking and start contemplating? Do you ever want to get off the roller-coaster of material life and just go within, and find that when you do you become aware of colours, sounds and smells that have eluded you before? And then you look at the world around you and know that it could all change if people would only change themselves? And a growing feeling of peace, positivity and goodness fills you, so much that you want to share it with others around you? And then you decide to become a psychic healer – oh, sorry, I've jumped ahead ...

You get the point. If you're one of those rare people who could not answer 'yes' to any of these questions, maybe there are other instances in your life which were just too definite to be chance. You think of someone you are not expecting to meet, and they walk round the corner at that exact instant. You pick up a thought from someone you are with when they utter the identical words you'd just had in mind. You think of someone at the moment they phone you, etc.

If you are still sceptical, are you sure it's not just plain cynicism? I know, I know – couldn't it all just be a series of coincidences?

Well, I have to admit that I am not a believer in coincidence. For one thing, it is just too unlikely. Certainly, due consideration should be given to the remote idea that everything happens by chance. But when a consistent pattern of events emerges which flies in the face of random occurrence; when they happen to you repeatedly; when they apply more when you are in a higher state of consciousness than when you are not; when they change your life – why resist the obvious? *According to the Law of Karma, there is no such thing as coincidence – there are only karmic incidents.*

Karma

The concept of Karma just rings true with people. It is one of the most ancient beliefs, and indeed words, on Earth. *Karma* is a Sanskrit term originally used in the Vedas of ancient India, which are dated by scholars as being over 5,000 years old, at least. Taking into account the fact that they were taught orally before they were ever written down, the teachings themselves could be tens or even hundreds of thousands of years old.

The teaching of Karma appears in one form or another in all major religions, Western as well as Eastern. It is the Judaic 'eye for an eye', the Christian 'as you sow, so shall you reap' and the Islamic concept of judgement. And yet in the 21st century, the original word, Karma, is still in common use – it has never been replaced. It is the subject of pop songs by John Lennon (*Instant Karma*), Boy George (*Karma Chameleon*), Radiohead (*Karma Police*), Robbie Williams (*Karma Killer*) and several rappers, I am told. There are Karma bracelets being sold in high street department stores in the West, as well as market places in the East, to bring the wearer luck. As I write this, there is even a Karma Cab company in London's West End to provide calmer and more peaceful journeys using aromatherapy and music! I am not endorsing all these things, or saying that they express the meaning of Karma correctly, but they are certainly an indication that, instinctively, people know that Karma is important. They realize that it makes sense of existence and human experience, and provides that most important of all things: a purpose to life.

Healers are practitioners of Karma Yoga, which is the greatest of all the branches of yoga. Most people think of yoga as being a form of physical exercise only, which is primarily used to keep fit or make you slimmer, or both. This is in fact Hatha Yoga, which is to be highly recommended but was devised originally as a preliminary for other, more important forms of yoga.

The word *yoga* literally means 'union with God', and this cannot be achieved at a purely physical level. The big four are Raja Yoga, which teaches oneness through meditation; Bhakti Yoga, which describes oneness through devotion and love; Gnani Yoga, where the path to follow comprises knowledge and wisdom; and Karma Yoga, where oneness is achieved through action and service to others. The healer can apply aspects of all these: meditation will induce a deeper sensitization, which is very useful in healing; love is a prerequisite for channelling the right kind of power; knowledge enables the healer to perfect his or her technique; and, above all, service is what healing really is. And it works at a karmic level, because the more you do for others through your healing work, the more you deserve to do, so the better a healer you become and the more you can achieve. It is a virtuous circle of spiralling growth. And it is most definitely, if you want it to be, a glorious path towards oneness with God.

I discovered just how many people are into Karma when I published my *Little Book of Karma* in 2000. It just took off. How popular is the idea that what goes around comes around? Do people want to accept that they get what they deserve? On the face of it you wouldn't think so, but like it or not, it just rings true with people. I had a rude awakening about this when discussing *Little Book of Karma* on a very popular Manchester radio phone-in. During the programme, which lasted four hours because the switchboard was jammed with callers, I was asked many questions, including how to deal with depression and cope with what seemed to be impossible situations. I could only reply that according to the philosophy of Karma, no matter how difficult a situation may seem, there is always a way; there is always something you can hang on to. That is the beauty of karmic philosophy – every situation can be sorted one way or another. There must be some lesson, some experience to be gained from everything, however bleak it may appear at the time.

What we did not know was that a woman in Manchester had decided to take her own life that night. She had lined up the pills on a shelf to perform their task and was ready to commit suicide, but decided to turn on the radio for one last time. She chose the exact moment that we were discussing the fact that there is always hope and a karmic purpose behind everything, no matter how bleak it may seem. As she listened (she told me later), she said it was as though a shaft of light entered the room and, as the host and I talked to more and more callers, this light became brighter and brighter. She threw away the pills and decided to live.

This showed me that, far from being a discouragement, the karmic ideal is a lifesaver. It was a final ray of hope for this woman, who realized the main thing of all: that there *is* a purpose, no matter how remote it may sometimes seem. Shortly afterwards there was a strange aftermath to this episode. I was discussing this incident a few days later with my good friend and top broadcaster Mike Allen on his late night show on LBC Radio in London. The well-known psychic Peter Walker was also in the studio. Shortly after describing this beautiful story, all three of us simultaneously saw what appeared to be a flash of light. Peter said he saw it travel from me to Mike; Mike and I just saw a bluish-white light. Coincidence or karmic incident? You decide.

Ten Top Karmic Tips

1   We all manipulate our own Karma for better or for worse, 24 hours a day.

2   Karma is designed to teach and help, not to punish or reward.

3   There are karmic signposts all around us – we just have to remove the blindfolds.

4   Karma is all-pervasive; it applies to every microbe, rock, plant, animal, human, planet, star, solar system, galaxy and beyond.

5   There is compassion within the Law, but only so much, or we would not learn the lessons of life.

6   Service to others is the most powerful way to improve your own Karma.

7   When you improve your own Karma, you improve the Karma of everything around you as well, to some degree.

8   Karma never gives you a challenge you cannot meet, despite all appearance to the contrary.

9   We can all change the world despite what the cynics may tell you.

10 Healing others is one of the finest ways to improve their Karma and yours.

Psychic Powers

If your motive is to help others and you make sufficient effort using correctly balanced techniques, then you will karmically deserve to develop psychic powers in one form or another. There is no better method of becoming psychic than giving healing, because this way the powers come to you naturally in an unforced, gentle fashion. You are allowing your latent potential to express itself in a controlled way.

The key to gaining this control is to start by working on your ability to concentrate. Concentration is the vital first step in mental development and yoga practice, which is too often missed out nowadays in classes on the subject. This will then gradually lead on to the ability to contemplate, which includes psychic awareness. While concentration enables you to focus single-mindedly on any object you choose, contemplation allows you to receive impressions at a psychic and mental level from the object. By learning concentration first, you will ensure the element of self-control over whatever psychic powers you tap into at a later stage.

Self-control is absolutely crucial in developing psychic powers. Uncontrolled psychic abilities can be more of a curse than a blessing because they can lead to mental instability. Psychics and psychologists should work together on this problem; in the future, I believe they will. There are deluded psychics who are mentally disturbed, and if you suffer from any form of mental illness it may not be wise to take up psychic development until you are better. But there are also people being diagnosed as mentally ill who are, in fact, having uncontrolled psychic experiences. That will never apply to you if you follow the methods taught in this book or another reliable and responsible source.

Keep a sense of humour, hang on to practical common sense and always remember that psychic powers are not given *to* you but *through* you. They are there to be used for the benefit of others as well as yourself, which is why healing makes such a perfect vehicle for them.

Psychic ability is as individual as taste in food, music, perfume or art. As banal as that may sound, it is in fact a very precise comparison, because psychic abilities are an extension of the senses. Contrary to certain Hollywood movies, there is no sixth sense *per se*. Psychic ability is an extension of the five physical senses: clairvoyance is psychic vision; clairaudience is psychic hearing; there also exist psychic smell, taste and touch. Then there is clairsentience, which is when you get a general feeling about things or pick up other people's moods. Whichever ability you are naturally inclined towards – and clairsentience is probably the most common – all manifest as apparently physical sensations.

There is a multitude of day-to-day expressions which indicate a physical response to a psychic impression: 'I've got a gut feeling,' 'I've got a funny taste in my mouth,' 'Something doesn't feel right,' 'This smells fishy' and even the somewhat unappealing 'I can feel it in my water'! All these expressions relate to tangible feelings, and there is a very good reason for this: There is a direct relationship between psychic impressions and physical sensations. The two are inseparably linked.

Although it is far from convincing when politicians utter platitudes such as 'I feel your pain,' there is some psychic sense in that statement. You can physically pick up symptoms from other people by experiencing a mirror image of what they are feeling. You will not pick up the actual ailment (unless it is contagious!), but if you are psychically attuned you can feel a minuscule degree of their pain.

You may have recognized this occurrence in your own life when doing the Health section of the Psychic Review, above. If so, it is vital that you are able to detach when necessary. If you are visiting a sick friend in hospital, you do not wish to pick up every sensation of pain along the way as you walk through the hospital or you will be in a pretty poor state by the time you reach your friend! That would be unlikely to happen, but you take my point. Nor should you use this ability to intrude into the privacy of another. You need to be able to switch these sensations on or off at will by deciding whether or not you wish to be in a receptive mood. Gradually your subconscious mind will learn to respond to the impulse it receives from your conscious decision to be attuned or otherwise.

But at times, and only with their consent, the ability to experience the physical or emotional state of another person can be very useful. As a healer, it can enable you to determine where the patient needs treatment most. It is also an invaluable tool for a counsellor. In fact, my own view is that, ideally, all counsellors should be psychically trained. I also think that all psychics should have some training in counselling, because it is quite possible, when giving guidance to others, to be psychically accurate but not truly helpful. You might empower someone to do something which is not in his or her best interests – psychic guidance is often self-fulfilling. I have given hundreds of psychic readings myself, but I must say that it is hard to know sometimes whether a person acted in a certain way partly because I told them they would. Hence the need for psychics to have counselling skills. But this type of attunement is essentially a very positive form of clairsentience, which you can use as a healer for the benefit of others.

As you develop your healing abilities, you will become more and more sensitive to your patients and will start to feel things about them. You will experience where they are at by feeling it – or a minuscule expression of it – firsthand. Psychic ability is about what you feel, not what you think, using the psychic attributes at your disposal.

The other five psychic abilities, based on each of the physical senses, can also be invaluable. Even at a purely physical level, the full mental interractions which take place when the senses are triggered are not completely understood by scientists. Of all the senses, the one which is probably understood least is the one most directly related to healing – namely, touch.

Drs Maggie Price and Gary Lewin[1] and colleagues unveiled in 2000 the discovery of a new protein which responds to the lightest touch. Known as brain sodium channel 1 (BNC1), or more colloquially the 'delicate touch' protein, it was discovered during research into a type of worm called *Caenorhabditis elegans* (you needed to know that!). Applying a gentle touch with an eyebrow hair glued to the end of a toothpick, scientists were able to pinpoint specific genes involved in touch, which are responsible for particular proteins. Their experiments continued with mice until they found the protein BNC1, which is linked to touch perception, and which has a human equivalent. This protein is not only present in the brain, but at the tips of the sensory nerves as well. The sensory nerves send out long fibres just below the skin which record hair movements. When the hair moves, the channels flip open and a signal is sent through the nerve fibre to the spinal cord and thence to the brain, which gets the message that the hair has moved.

There is no reason why such signals should not also be transmitted at a supersensory level through psychic channels to the brain – hence the term extrasensory perception (ESP).

Additional research has been performed into the links between the different physical senses. For example, Emiliano Macaluso[2] of University College London, working with Professor Chris Frith and Professor Jon Driver, discovered that activating the sense of touch can also boost the ability of a person to respond to a light stimulus. There can be a similar interchange between the psychic senses, and so it is possible that you will develop some other form of psychic ability through healing, such as clairvoyance or clairaudience. It may just happen to you one day, as if it were the most ordinary thing in the world. In fact, it may be triggered by your healing work, which has unleashed inner powers.

When I first experienced clairvoyance, I had been giving healing for several years. It seemed completely natural at the time: I could just see someone else in the room, as though I was imagining them. When I described them in detail to the person I was with, I found that it was an exact description of someone they had known and who had died some years earlier. This started me on my personal psychic quest. As a healer, you may start to 'see' the psychic colours around a patient. This can be very useful in guiding you to where the treatment is needed. I have been amazed at just how many people with the right guidance can see another person's aura in classes I have run in Britain and the US. If clairvoyance should develop naturally within you, then allow it to do so. It will come in useful in your healing work.

Clairaudience is less common, but can be very useful indeed. It is generally used to communicate with guides or guardian angels, who may offer you help in your healing work.

It is of course vital that you learn to tell the difference between your imagination and a genuine message. If you receive a clairaudient message, you may not know in the early stages what it is. A thought may pop into your head, which turns out to be right. Did a guide put it there, or did it come from your own intuition? In some ways it does not matter, as long as it is correct. But you may find that with that thought comes a sound, an intonation and even possibly an accent with a voice. This is clairaudience. Until you are proficient, always keep (and this may surprise you) a degree of scepticism: it could be your imagination. Even if it is clairaudience, it is essential to maintain full control and not to enter some kind of trance, thereby allowing the entity to take over your consciousness.

I am sorry to say that not all communicating entities are benign. The more you know about this work, the more complex it becomes. It is vital in the early stages of clairaudience to be cautious and discriminating. If in doubt, just put the experience on a mental shelf until it is proved one way or the other.

There is nothing wrong with having a psychic experience and not knowing exactly what it means. Too many psychics jump to erroneous conclusions, instead of keeping an open mind until they are certain. In time, if you are meant to go in a clairaudient direction, you will know the difference between your imagination, your intuition, and guidance from an outside source. They will just feel completely different.

Psychic smell and taste are more rare. Some healers develop an acute sense of smell, and can tell from this the physical condition of a patient and what type of healing they require. I have met only two practitioners of psychic taste, and they both used it as a form of clairsentience. The experience of a specific taste, like the much-quoted 'funny taste in my mouth', can lead to a general feeling about people or situations.

Finally there is psychic touch, in which some people are able, through the practice of psychometry, to 'read' from a physical object things about its owner or history. This is something anyone can learn to do, and it is certainly a 'fun' thing, too.

The best expression of psychic touch is, of course, healing. Psychic touch is one ability you are guaranteed to become proficient in if you practise the techniques in this book sufficiently. As far as the others go, we are all different. Some develop several of them; some do not need to. It all depends on what you need for your healing work.

Psychic abilities should never be treated, as they too often are, as party tricks. Nor do they work too well in an academic environment. In some cases, psychics working in parapsychology experiments in universities have obtained worse and worse results as the experiments continued. There are two reasons for this, I believe. First, because psychic abilities are based on feelings, they respond to atmosphere and mood. Academic environments are not always the most conducive to psychic work. Secondly, they are meant to be spiritual abilities used in service to others, rather than for intellectual speculation, no matter how well meaning it may be. They just work better when genuinely helpful work is being done.

Healing is far more important than damaging cutlery, or even walking on water, for that matter. Developing psychic abilities for the purpose of helping others provides its own in-built protection: it will of itself tend to attract the interest of benign, spiritual influences. You will develop psychic powers in a gradual, unforced fashion, as and when you need them. 'Vive la différence!', as they say in France. We all have the same psychic potential, but we each develop it in different ways depending on our own innate attributes. I will develop this topic further in Chapter 6.

Our psychic being is comprised of subtle universal life-forces. These were discussed in detail in the previous chapter as existing on many frequencies of matter to produce manifestations within the ethers of space. These universal life-forces have been known by many names, the most common being *prana* (in yoga philosophy) and *chi* (in Chinese healing methods and martial arts systems). It is these you may have already experienced in the Three Energy Tests in Chapter 1. And it is these which you will use as the energy source for your healing.

Here are some tests you can use to feel, as a direct physical sensation, this natural healing power. You will need to use your faculty of imagination by visualizing this energy as white light. White is used because it contains all colours of the spectrum, and therefore includes whichever colour vibration you need at a particular time.

Feeling Healing Power

Inspiration

Sit with your spine straight on a hard-backed chair. Close your eyes and become aware of your breathing. You will probably find that it is rather irregular. You may also find that you are using only a fraction of your lung capacity. Try to use the whole of your diaphragm as well as your chest, allowing your stomach area to expand slightly on the in-breath, and to pull inwards on the out-breath. Now place your hands on top of each other on your stomach area, just above your navel, where the solar plexus centre is located in the aura.

As you breathe in, visualize white light entering you, not just through your nostrils but from above your head as well. This energy flows throughout the cosmos in an inexhaustible supply – it just requires you to invoke it.

On the out-breath, visualize the light travelling down both your arms through the palms of your hands and into the solar plexus region. See if you start to feel a tingling sensation throughout your body or heat in the palms of your hands and stomach region. If you do, it is the energy you have literally breathed into yourself. The literal meaning of the word *inspiration* is, after all, 'to breathe in'.

All Fingers and Elbows

Follow the same procedure, but instead of placing your hands on your stomach, take your left thumb between the thumb and fingers of your right hand. Then start the same breathing and visualizing process in the previous exercise, but instead of sending the energy into your solar plexus, send it from your right hand through your left thumb and into your left arm. It is as though you have created an energy circuit going round and round. After a while you should start to feel some tingling in your left elbow, where the circuit is generally a little blocked by the elbow's awkward position. If not, you may feel some of the sensations of the previous exercise.

One on One

To do this exercise you will need someone who is open-minded to work with. Sit facing each other with your hands downwards on your knees. Each of you should practise deep breathing and visualize white light entering your bodies on the in-breath. Now raise your right hand while your partner raises their left hand exactly in front of your right, but an inch or two away. Continue the breathing as before, but now send the energy from one raised palm to the other on the out-breath. After a while you should both feel at least some tingling and possibly some heat. You may even feel a shaft of white light entering you from an outside source.

This is the easiest of the three exercises to get a result from, since two people working together are more than twice as powerful as one working alone, providing they both try with an open mind.

You will probably have obtained a result with at least one of these exercises, which will show you that you can sense the energy you will need to use. If you have not, do not be discouraged; sooner or later you will.

The next step is to fashion this energy with your love so that it becomes a dynamic force for healing. *The science of the healing technique has to be tempered by the love, your love, with which you apply it.* Only then will it work miracles.

Psychic energy has to become transformed into love energy. If there were one qualification for a healer, it would not be how psychic they are but how much love they have for their fellow humans — and for animals and plants, for that matter. We can all pay lip service to how much love we feel for others; the only thing that really counts is what we *do* about it. Results, results, results are the measure of greatness. They are also the true expression of the soul.

The Soul Urge

It was the Stoic Roman philosopher Seneca, trapped in the employment of that most infamous of bosses, Nero, who pointed out that 'the soul alone raises us to nobility.' In the midst of an evil empire as corrupt and deceitful as ancient Rome, Seneca could see clearly that true nobility was a spiritual virtue. Despite his admonition that the root of all unhappiness was disappointment caused by raising one's expectations too high, leading to a somewhat pessimistic philosophy of life, Seneca could still hold an idealistic view of the soul. In this, he concurs with all the major and most of the minor religious philosophies of the world. It is this *soul urge* that drives people to a universal love of all life, providing it has a vehicle for expression, such as healing. Then the psychic frustrations, of which you were possibly not even aware, will be stripped away and you will discover a newfound sense of freedom.

Amid all the talk of sexual and emotional repression, something even more significant to the human psyche has got lost: soul repression. The soul urge is at least as strong, potentially, as the sexual urge; it is just much more deeply buried in most people. And yet it is still not socially acceptable to talk too freely about it.

The soul is exciting, stimulating, ecstatic, but you wouldn't think so from the way it is presented. Religions are relegated, for the most part, to two main functions: to comfort the dead and cement the family – both worthwhile tasks, but only a tiny fraction of the potential of the soul.

But the soul is stirring within, demanding change, action and new priorities. When you give healing, you will tap into a pure, impersonal love for all things animate and inanimate, which is there within you just waiting to be expressed. When you light the fire of the soul, it ignites in a firmament of psychic power and healing energy. It changes you for the better. And the results are plain to see in the faces of those you have healed. Because, above all, the soul is urging us to act.

Song of the Soul

The soul is alive, so revive it.
The Love of all life is asleep, so awaken it.
The purpose is clear, so follow it.
The dream is inspired, so manifest it.
The spiritual vision can be attained, so go for it.
Indifference is hesitating;
Lethargy is debilitating;
Selfishness is terminating –
And he who terminates is lost.
But not for ever,
For the soul will sing its song of renewal again.
The time has come, so take it.
The power is there, so use it.
The experience is yours, so learn it.
The result is divine, so praise it.
The soul is alive, so let it sing.

There are few on Earth who have attained full soul consciousness, which is also known as cosmic consciousness. One of these was the master of yoga I was fortunate enough to know and learn from, Dr George King. He applied his superconscious awareness to the study of natural healing and how it really works. In the next chapter I will tell you more about this amazing man, to whom I was very fortunate to be a close friend, disciple and colleague for over 20 years.

3 *Analysis of a Yogi*

According to Tibetan Buddhists, a teacher should not be chosen so much for his communication skills, as for the fact that he has demonstrated in his own life the lesson he is teaching. Such a person, said the Tibetans, may not be the best speaker, but has the power to convey the essence of the teaching far more effectively than the most eloquent person who has not lived what he is teaching. It is something we all instinctively want from teachers: that they practise what they preach. If you had the choice of learning to paint from a brilliant artist who had demonstrated her skills over and over again, but had poor grammar and little speaking ability, or from someone who was not a very good artist but had read numerous books on the subject and could communicate fluently, whom would you go to? The answer is obvious. So, when I wanted to learn how to heal, I went to Dr George King. Fortunately for me, he had both experience and eloquence.

George King

If experience is the key ingredient for a teacher, the recipe for healing lay literally in Dr King's hands. Most of the substance of this book is made up of the teaching Dr King passed on to me. His hallmark was to share his experience as far as he possibly could with others. He had demonstrated the highest known meditative states and many psychic and spiritual powers, and had committed himself to empowering others to demonstrate their latent abilities, particularly in the fields of healing and prayer. From the 1950s until his demise in 1997, Dr King taught thousands to become healers at a time when it was not fashionable, even within the healing movement, to believe that anyone could do it. Healing power was considered to be a gift – you either had it or you didn't. Eventually, people started to accept the concept he had pioneered for so long in the simple but life-changing catchphrase: *You too can heal!*

In a much smaller way, I know how this feels. My first book about psychic development was inspired by Dr King's empowering approach, and was dedicated to him. When it was published in 1993 under the title *Unlock Your Psychic Powers*, it was still a controversial idea that anyone could become psychic. Since then, there have been many other books with a similar theme to mine – some even with similar cover designs! The word 'Unlock' has been used unsparingly to release a whole variety of inner attributes. And that is fine, as long as the authors know from practical experience what they are teaching. Otherwise it would be a case of the partially sighted leading the visually challenged, and that would only lead to one thing: seriously impaired vision!

No one among the hundreds of healers and alternative practitioners I have met have understood how healing works better than Dr King. So in this chapter I will quote freely from his writings, which are based primarily on yoga philosophy, as well as his own realizations as a yogi in his own right. I see no point in trying to re-invent the wheel when the basic philosophy of healing has already been brilliantly expressed by someone who knew from firsthand experience exactly what he was teaching. Lengthy tracts have been written in academic and verbose language on this subject, which really all boil down to some simple and straightforward facts. Scientists could save themselves a lot of time and speculation if they learned from ancient, yogic wisdom. Of course they could develop further applications for these concepts, and I am sure they will, but the basic philosophy is simple. I will put Dr King's words in italics to distinguish them from my own more detailed commentaries.

The Five Elements

It was known by the Wise Ones, thousands of years ago, that the Universal Life Forces impregnated all matter in Creation. That as far as this Planet is concerned, these Universal Life Forces emanated from the Sun, the Moon and other bodies in space close to us, but the major source was the Sun. The Ancients referred to them as 'pranas'.

There are five major pranas and five minor pranas. A major prana flows for a period of 32 minutes and then is replaced by another form which flows for another 32 minutes throughout the whole five aspects of prana. In the meantime, the five minor pranas also flow for 32-minute periods and they are inter-blended into the major pranas, so as to support all life as we know it. If you amalgamate the pranas together in one way, the result must be a piece of lead. If you amalgamate the pranas together in another way, the result would be a gold nugget; even in a different way, the oxygen in the air you breathe; a different way still, the chlorophyll which makes plant-life green.

The number five is very significant throughout metaphysical philosophy, linking directly to the five physical and psychic senses. All creation, say the yogis, is composed of five qualities, called *tattvas*, each of which relates to a different flow of *prana*, a different sense and a different expression of life in all its forms. In Western magical practice, each *tattva* would be termed as one of the five mystical elements – not to be confused with the chemical elements, which are an entirely different thing.

These five mystical elements form the basis of Western mystical traditions and many systems of divination. In the tarot pack, which is reputed to have originated in Egypt, for example, there are four suits – swords, wands, hearts and pentacles – known as the minor arcana, and another set of 22 cards comprising the major arcana. The first four suits are the basic four elements: earth, air, fire, and water, though which suit applies to which element is hotly disputed. The fifth element – ether – is represented by the major arcana, which significantly number 22 cards, itself a master number in the practice of numerology.

Back in the world of everyday game-playing, the ordinary set of playing cards has done away with the major arcana, leaving only four suits – spades, diamonds, hearts and clubs. Almost by accident, they have kept one esoteric card in the pack, though it is hardly used – this is the joker, which is arguably the most mystical card of all.

Thinking about it, there could be a metaphor here for materialistic life: the mystical potential exists, but it is largely ignored, misunderstood and completely under-estimated – but let's not get negative about an ordinary pack of playing cards. The joker card is, in fact, based on the Fool card in the major arcana of the tarot pack. He is depicted with one foot on the ledge of a cliff and the other in mid-air, as though he is walking over the edge. At first sight he is a complete idiot who will fall to his death; but to the mystic he is about to transcend matter and fly off the cliff.

This idea of someone who appears to be a fool, but is actually the wisest man around, was very familiar in Western courts, who usually had a jester (hence joker) among their number. Shakespeare, for example, under the influence (and possibly the pen, by some accounts) of the Rosicrucian Grand Master and mystic, Sir Francis Bacon, often attributes telling perceptions to his fools.

In astrology, the elements are clear in their original form: Taurus, Virgo and Capricorn are earth signs; Aquarius, Gemini and Libra are air signs; Aries, Leo and Sagittarius are fire signs; and Pisces, Cancer and Scorpio are water signs. The mystical fifth element of ether is taken to be the crucial element of interpretation performed by the astrologer on a chart. After all, different people will respond differently to similar charts, as in the case of twins, and individual interpretation is always necessary.

Alchemists were always striving to discover this mysterious fifth element, not for the purpose of transmuting metal into gold, but in order to transmute matter spiritually onto a higher plane of existence. This was the secret behind the so-called 'philosopher's stone' and the ability to store information in objects such as the fabled emerald tablet of hermetic writings. All these quests strove to discover the ability to harness the universal life-forces and use them for a variety of mystical purposes.

Pranayama

In alchemy, physical objects and materials were often used as focuses for harnessing the universal life-forces, whereas in yoga philosophy the physical and psychic body of the practitioner were generally the main focus. The main method used in yogic practice was *Pranayama*, a system of yoga breathing devised to charge yourself up with universal life-forces by drawing them into your aura and chakras on the air you breathe. Advanced practitioners, particularly in the past, would specifically target individual *pranas* and *tattvas* by picking particular times to perform their exercises. They would know that at those times they would be able to draw the particular aspect of the five major and minor pranas they needed for a particular purpose. For most of us this would not be possible in our busy lives, even if we knew exactly what aspect of *prana* was flowing when. But if you are really keen, there is one simple way to ensure that you get the particular aspect of *prana* you need at any one time. If you perform *Pranayama* for 2 hours and 40 minutes (160 minutes), you will guarantee to get all the major and minor *pranas*, because that is an exact multiple of 32 minutes times 5 – the length of time a complete flow of all major and minor *pranas* takes. I have done this myself and can recommend it.

In certain ancient schools of yoga, the secret of breath was regarded as the secret of life. The correct control of the in-breath in relation to the out-breath, and in particular holding the breath in (known as *Kumbhaka*) for lengthy periods of time, or sometimes holding it out, could be used to induce all the major powers. These included extending physical as well as psychic hearing, having an outstanding capacity for memory, and entering a deep state of meditation (*samyama*) which enables the meditator to take on any object of choice. A *samyama* brings such a oneness with that object that the meditator virtually knows it from the inside, and, at times, assumes its characteristics. A *samyama* could, for example, literally give you the strength of an elephant or the agility of a cat, because you would literally take on the characteristics of those animals by performing a deep meditation upon them.

Astral projection, levitation and invisibility could all be attained purely through *Pranayama* – Dr King himself demonstrated this latter ability while attending a seminar in Brighton in the 1950s. However, it is certainly not necessary to go to these lengths or to attain these powers in order to become a healer. All the *pranas* are beneficial, and a few minutes of regular deep breathing as described in Chapter 2 will suffice. A balanced system of breathing exercises can only be recommended, and if you choose to do this you can get more information from the contact details in the Appendix to this book, or by contacting a reliable yoga centre in your area.

Seven: The Number of Spirituality

So it can be seen that the five major pranas and the five minor pranas are not only flowing consistently throughout the day and night in and through all life forms, but are absolutely vital to all material life forms. The pranas, like all other aspects of Creation, exist in a seven-dimensional framework and they too have their more subtle aspects.

While five is the number of energy, seven is regarded as the number of spirituality. Mystics have known for centuries that there are six levels of existence higher than the physical one on which we live, making a total of seven planes. All energies vibrate throughout the spectrum of these levels. But the seven dimensions Dr King refers to are something else. Together, they define the framework in which we as sentient beings gain experience. This question of the dimensions is such a vast and profound philosophical subject that I can only give the briefest of summaries here.

As mentioned in Chapter 1, this is one of the foremost areas of scientific enquiry at the present time – and rightly so. As long ago as the 1950s, Dr King published his concept of the seven dimensions of creation based on his contacts with higher spiritual beings than himself.

The first four dimensions were already well established then: *length*, *breadth*, *height* and *time*. Dr King described the fifth dimension as *motion* – it is, after all, the movement of planetary bodies which determines time. His concept of the sixth dimension was more controversial: *mind*. He said that there is a mind behind all things, including creation itself, which applies from the macrocosm to the microcosm and the animate to the inanimate. Dr King asserted that there is a mind behind a sun, just as there is behind a wooden chair, and it is this mind which brings together the necessary energies to hold it in being. There are numerous reports of mechanical objects behaving as though they react to feelings as well as technological factors – from motor cars responding differently to different drivers for no apparent reason, to the atmosphere you discover in a new home.

The seventh dimension propounded by Dr King is more contentious still for some people: *divine will*. In common with yoga philosophy, he said that within us all is a divine spark, which operates through an innate sense of will which is beyond even mind. It is in fact the soul urge which I described earlier, which is attempting to move us in a spiritual direction. The soul urge can be just as starved of spiritual food as a homeless person might be of a physical meal. It wants to join in battle against spiritual poverty, if only we will let it.

Investigations into the function of the brain have shown that before we take any physical action, or even mental action, some other type of impulse has been generated through the nervous system. Experiments designed to measure the relationship between the brain and nervous system have, on occasions, brought unexpected results. In certain cases, apparatus being used to measure a person's physical responses registered an internal reaction milliseconds before the brain itself was activated. This unexpected result was interpreted by some as being the impulse of the soul.

The Breath of Life

Pranas blended in one way, help the cells in your body to continually reproduce; blended in another way, they help the cells in your aura to continually reproduce.

… If you go without breath for a few minutes, your body will die and you, the mind and Spirit, will have to leave it. If you go without drinking for a few days, the same thing will happen to your physical structure; without eating for a few weeks, again the same thing will happen to it.

... of the three, breathing is the most important energy intake. In fact, the Yogis say that your Karmic pattern, when you came to Earth in the present incarnation, was governed by so many in-breaths and so many out-breaths. If you take these in-breaths as short quick breaths, as most people do, you will not live as long as if you make them long and deep, retaining the energy within the body as long as possible before expulsion of the toxic matter which leaves the body through the out-breath.

It is taught in *Pranayama* that the deeper you breathe, the deeper you are capable of thinking. This is because you do not just inhale oxygen, but the universal life-forces, which feed your chakras and nadic system and enable more profound realizations. Interestingly, wisdom was not regarded in the East as an intellectual ability or even an accumulation of knowledge, though both of these would be by-products of it. Wisdom was essentially looked upon as a state of being. In a higher state of consciousness you would be capable of wise conclusions; in a lower one, no matter how sharp your brain or how well-versed your intellect, your conclusions would be suspect. This is epitomized by the old saying that a person can be 'too clever by half' – and we all know the difference between a clever person and a wise one.

Breathing correctly can alter your mental condition in a number of other ways as well. For example, if you ensure that the length of your in-breath is as equal as possible to the length of your out-breath, you will tend to become a more balanced person and better able to deal with the stresses and strains of life.

If you have a regularly blocked nose, this too will affect you. Energies breathed in through the left nostril tend to be associated with a calm and peaceful condition, whereas those breathed in through the right nostril tend to induce a more proactive and dynamic state. You can balance out a blocked nasal condition by ensuring that you breathe for a few minutes through the obstructed nostril – at least mentally, if it is not possible physically. This will at least draw the *pranas* to you, even though you cannot inhale air.

Energized Foods

In order to get food and drink which is as energized as possible with *prana*, avoid processed products as much as possible. Water taken directly from a spring would be ideal, but is hardly accessible to most of us nowadays. Fresh fruit juices, though, taken from organically grown fruit, is excellent for obtaining *prana* as well as benefiting from their natural nutritional value. This is not a book on diet, but it goes without saying that if you can get the vitamins and minerals you need from natural foods rather than supplements, it is much better. What is not so well known is that one of the main reasons for this is that natural foods have a much stronger charge of universal life-forces.

The Aura

Just as your physical structure needs a balanced energy intake, so also does your auric structure. Unlike the physical structure though, the aura does not breathe as such, does not take drink as such, and does not eat as such; and yet it does take in and expel energy and toxic materials rather in the same way as you do with the out-breath and eliminatory canal system.

Around the physical body we all have a psychic counterpart called the *aura*. This is in fact an energy body containing a psychic reflection of the physical body, though it might be truer to say that the physical is a reflection of the psychic.

The exact distance of the aura or psychic energy body from the physical body varies from person to person. Tradition has it that the Lord Buddha had an aura of 40 square miles, which is taken to illustrate the colossal spiritual influence of this great master. Generally, it is a few inches away from the physical body and forms an ovoid shape. When you are able to see it psychically, it can appear to follow the contours of the body. This can look like a yellow or golden light around the person you are looking at, which is not the full aura, but just an etheric reflection of the physical body. If it grows and expands, revealing other colours and patterns, then you are seeing the aura itself.

It is important to distinguish between a psychic vision of the body and the photoelectric effect, which is a purely physical phenomenon. When you look at an object and then look away, you can often see what seems to be a transparent image of that object in the sky or wherever you are looking. This is a photoelectric image caused by the eyes, which soon fades away. A clairvoyant vision of the aura does the exact opposite – instead of fading away, it seems to grow and expand before your vision as you are able to see more and more of it.

It is not necessary to be clairvoyant, though, to detect a person's aura. We all know how it feels to be in the presence of a dynamic, charismatic person – energy is radiated all around them for better or for worse. Our mental, emotional and physical condition is contained within the aura as pools of energy, manifesting as colour. A clairvoyant may see these and be able to determine our state of mind. Hence the old joke that when two clairvoyants meet they ask each other not 'How are you?' but 'How am I?'! One thing that giving healing will do for you, even though it should never be your motive for doing so, will be to cleanse and improve the condition of your own aura. By being a channel for healing energy to be radiated to others, a natural cleansing will take place of your aura as the energy passes through you.

Psychic Centres

The aura takes in and expels energy through little floodgates or power vortices in different parts of its body. These are referred to as 'Chakras' in Sanskrit or as 'psychic centres' in the English language.

Reference to Illustration 1 will show you the positions of the [seven major psychic centres, as well as the vitally important psychic centres in the palms of the hands]. Each one of these has a different function, [and] uses different energies for different purposes. But the total amalgamation of this energy intake and output is absolutely essential to material existence.

Within the aura are a number of psychic nerve centres, or chakras, which are crucial to the healing process. These are linked by an interconnecting series of psychic channels known as *nadis* or the nadic system. According to some Eastern writings, there are no fewer than 72,000 of these nadis.

The simple act of shaking hands is, in fact, a transference of psychic energy between the psychic centres in the palms of the hands. The Eastern practice of bowing with the hands flat against each other was intended to hold the positive energy within as a gesture of respect. When you get 'butterflies in the stomach' because you are nervous, it is often because the solar plexus centre, which is effectively your battery for the reception and radiation of *prana*, has become activated. Similarly, when you are in the presence of a hostile or demanding person, you can often feel depletion in this area. Once you are aware of the existence and function of these centres, you will be far more sensitive to their activity in day-to-day life.

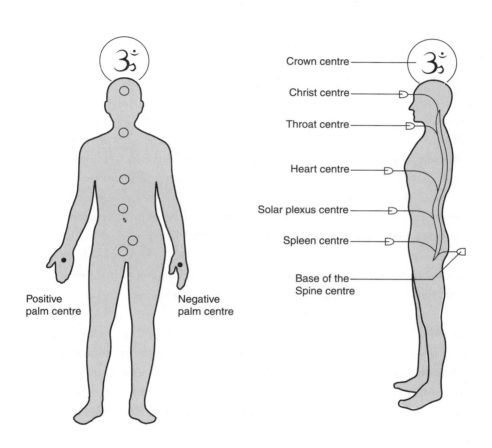

Illustration 1: The Nine Psychic Centres

In general, the higher centres are neglected in favour of the lower ones, which is a mark of the unspiritual, emotionally-driven lives that many people choose to live. As you take up the practice of healing, you will gradually, in an unforced fashion, increasingly start to activate the higher centres. As you do so, you will become sensitive to psychic and spiritual activities you never thought possible before, and which are in fact far more satisfying in a lasting sense than the lower ones. That is not to say that the lower centres are in any way wrong, it is just that they are over-used by most of us to the detriment of the higher ones.

Some yoga writings frown on the lower psychic centres. This is incorrect: all the centres are absolutely essential. It is a question of redressing the balance, not of eliminating any aspect of the human psyche. Giving healing will do this for you at both a spiritual level and, even more importantly, at a karmic level, because your motive will always be to help others first and foremost. Because the personal benefits in terms of spiritual development will be a secondary consideration, they will be all the surer. One aspect of Karma is that whatsoever you reject will be laid at your feet. Because you have put service to others above your own spiritual development, your evolution will be all the more certain.

You may have noticed one deliberate error in Dr King's depiction of the major psychic centres — namely the omission of the sex centre and the addition of the spleen centre in its place. This is not done in any way to minimize the truth, but purely for practical reasons. When it comes to laying the hands on the individual psychic centres, as described in detail in Chapter 5, it would be inappropriate and quite possibly illegal to use the sex centre. That is the main reason, though Dr King did add that this is one centre which is over-used anyway, and therefore hardly in need of energy. Far be it from me to comment!

Dis-Ease

... if any [of these psychic centres] is in any way inhibited by damage to the aura, to the subtle nervous systems, or even the physical systems, then discomfort or 'dis-ease' results. Some 'dis-eases' start within the physical body and are reflected out into the aura. Some termed 'psychosomatic diseases' start in the aura or psychic centres and have their reflection in the denser cellular structure of the physical body.

The medical community defines 'psychosomatic illness' in a narrow manner, as bodily symptoms caused by mental or emotional disturbance. Dr King used the term to include an auric cause of illness as well as a mental or emotional one.

The relationship between the aura and the physical body is very much two-way. Even an accidental injury such as a broken leg will cause a discolouration of the aura. By working directly on the aura of a patient through healing, you can affect all illnesses whether starting in the aura or the physical body. Once the auric aspect of the illness is healed, it will reflect onto the physical body as good health. That is why there is no such thing as an ailment which cannot be treated successfully by healing. There are patients who are very difficult to heal because of karmic factors and because of their negative attitudes, which become self-fulfilling, but every ailment can be helped through healing.

A Holistic Approach

Healing is a truly holistic approach to health. It does not just look at the whole person physically, but psychically as well. Instead of analysing the mental and emotional background of the patient psychologically – though that will come into any guidance you give, as covered in detail in Chapter 7 – healing works directly at an energy level, and so can affect all types of illness and disease. At this level, physical, mental and emotional factors are all merged into one. If the psychic imbalance is rectified at an auric level, harmony will prevail through the whole being of the patient. If this rectification is complete, and providing the patient does not re-introduce a discolouration of the aura – through negative thinking, for example – the patient will in time be completely cured.

Some expert healers, who are able to see the aura, can make a very exact diagnosis of a physical ailment by seeing its outward reflection in the subtle bodies or the incorrect working of a psychic centre. Medical science tends to study the effect, namely the reflection in the physical body, and treat that effect without always being aware of the cause, which may well be a 'psychosomatic condition' started by contamination or damage to the aura. Wrong thought patterns will also affect the aura in such a way as to cause a psychosomatic condition, which can adversely affect the physical body.

It is not necessary or recommended for a healer to be able to psychically diagnose a patient. Simple questioning is quite sufficient to enable you to perform a healing treatment. However, some healers have a natural aptitude for picking up ailments, and I will cover this in detail in Chapter 6. Aura-reading is increasingly popular, but requires a high degree of proficiency to practise correctly. Some training courses are superficial, to say the least – it is always well to remember, in psychic work, Alexander Pope's great maxim that 'a little learning is a dangerous thing.'
A clairvoyant may see a discolouration of the aura around the abdomen of a patient, for example, and immediately deduce that it is cancerous when it is in fact a digestive problem. As irresponsible as this may sound, I have come across cases like this.

In the early stages of psychic development, it can be so exciting to discover your fantastic untapped inner potential that you over-estimate your abilities. Another great maxim that I often quote is Socrates' statement that he was the wisest man in Athens because he knew what he did not know. Often you will not know exactly how to interpret something you sense or feel psychically – if so, it is vital that you recognize this. There is always a pressure on psychics to explain themselves. Sceptics and cynics tend to demand absolute, clear definitions of what a psychic is asserting so that they can assess it or demolish it accordingly. You do not have to answer to sceptics or cynics – they have their place, but it is generally not a very creative one. Just stay with what you know and what you do not know. If you detect either visually, by touch, or through another psychic sense some imbalance in a patient's aura, there is no obligation upon you to declare immediately exactly what you think their condition is.

Successful Healing

It is ... the intimate interrelationship between the aura, the psychic centres, the subtle nerve centres, the physical nervous system, and the physical body, that makes Spiritual Healing so successful.

'Dis-ease' or discomfort is brought about by some wrong function of either the mental or physical workings of man, or the workings of the psychic centres. Even so, if the psychic centres all worked perfectly as they should, then even a malignant disease such as cancer would be removed from the physical body by the impingement of subtle forces upon its molecular and atomic structure.

This is really a perfect definition of what healing is and why it works. Every hospital should have healers working in it; every doctor's surgery should utilize healers alongside other forms of medical treatment; every complementary medical practice should incorporate healing. As dogmatic as this may sound, I believe it to be true and have campaigned for over 20 years in Britain to have healing on the National Health Service together with other natural methods of medicine. It should not be the only type of treatment, but it should be one of the indispensable ones, because it works in a unique way.

Certainly, some forms of acupressure and acupuncture tap into the meridians, which I believe reflect upon the psychic nervous system. Homoeopathy also works, I believe, at a subtle level – hence the need to succuss the remedies. But psychic healing is the only comprehensive form of auric treatment, in which I of course include related systems under different names such as Spiritual, Natural, Yogic, Pranic and Reiki Healing, Chi Kung and others. The name matters not a jot – the approach is vital to the future of medicine.

Picture yourself as a Spiritual being controlling your complex mental, auric and physical structure; that through your aura, great forces are entering in a subtle state and impressing the brain of you so that it can receive and translate mind impulses. You have complete control of all these forces and if you need more of theses forces to perform any function, you can immediately call on them by deep breathing, by attracting them to yourself by the right thought, whether that thought be unexpressed or expressed as it is, for instance, in Prayer or Mantra, and you can make yourself into a veritable power house. So powerful, in fact, that you can afford to give this life energy to one less fortunate than yourself who is suffering disharmony, discomfort or as most people call it – disease.

... Outside of you now, from the surface of this Globe way beyond the Sun, is your storehouse of tremendous natural forces. Bring these into yourself and then you can greatly help your suffering brother.

Enough said – the theory is clear, now for the practice! First you need to prepare yourself to become a powerful channel for healing powers, by developing what I have called 'the yin of calm and the yang of charisma'.

4 *The Yin of Calm and the Yang of Charisma*

Healing energy can be expressed in a multitude of different ways – depending upon the mindset of the healer who is channelling it. There is a constant interchange of energy taking place between human beings, and indeed all living things, for better or for worse. The healer deliberately conditions this energy with his or her love. Healing is something you can do throughout your life, wherever you go. So how do you become a channel for healing energies?

Developing a Healing Presence

'First cometh the angel, peace to make way for the goddess, love. Open up the door, let peace enter in, then will come the other in splendour to live forever within your soul.' These wonderful words, which were channelled by an elevated master through Dr King,[1] speak for themselves. How can you radiate peace to others, if you do not first feel it within yourself? The twinfold themes of love and peace received bad publicity during the hippie days of the late 1960s, often being confused with sex and drugs. But although the idea of 'love and peace' has been much mocked, it still stands as the main foundation of spirituality. This and this alone can save humanity from self-destruction, and with enough of both, humanity will be saved.

The inner life always manifests in the outside world sooner or later, and vice versa – as the Chinese taught thousands of years ago in their superb philosophy of *yin* (inner life) and *yang* (outer life). The ancient Chinese developed a whole way of life based upon these two balancing forces of yin and yang, epitomized in their wonderful book of divination and wisdom, the *I Ching*, which literally means 'Book of Changes'. This is a work composed of 64 symbolic writings called hexagrams which, between them, are said to answer all the questions which life presents at different moments in our evolution.

Each hexagram is symbolically described by a combination of two different types of lines – one solid, one broken. Every hexagram has six of these lines, and there are 64 possible combinations of these two types of lines. These 64 hexagrams were traditionally found by throwing yarrow stalks for each line and, depending how each stalk fell, it would be considered solid or broken. Nowadays they are generally found by tossing three coins, with a majority of heads representing solid lines, and a majority of tails representing broken lines.

The basic principle behind the I Ching – as with the tarot, the runes, palmistry and other forms of divination – is that nothing happens by chance. Just as tarot cards are said to fall in a particular way by design, so the hexagram is achieved by karmic determination, not the haphazard throwing of coins. (This book is not the place to go into the minutiae of I Ching interpretation, however, a subject upon which many books have been written – see the Bibliography).

The concept behind the I Ching is the balance of these two forces: the broken line being yin, and the solid line yang. When taken in their purest form, as six of each (either solid or broken lines) in one hexagram, you get the essence of that aspect of energy. In the case of yang, which is the first hexagram in the I Ching, it is *Ch'ien* or 'The Creative', and in the case of yin, the second hexagram, it is *K'un* or 'The Receptive'.

The sage Confucius, whose name is still synonymous with wisdom, dedicated the latter part of his life to interpreting and commenting upon the I Ching. Although he lived around 500 BC, the exact age of the I Ching itself is unknown. The first ancient collection that we know of is dated from the period of the Hsia Dynasty which, according to tradition, lasted from 2205 to 1766 BC – it could be far older than that, though. The collection which Confucius is said to have worked from originated in the Shang Dynasty, which is dated from 1766 to 1150 BC. Interestingly, this edition started with the hexagram *K'un*, 'The Receptive', which fits in with the idea of yin coming before yang. Of course, in reality neither can really precede the other, because each is dependent upon the other.

Running through the I Ching is the idea, also very prevalent in Lao-Tzu's *Tao Te Ching* and generally in the philosophy of Taoism, that everything on the surface is in a state of constant change, but underlying it is constancy. That which is constant is the only reality. By understanding and becoming one with change, you can move beyond it into that which is unchangeable, the lasting reality of ultimate truth. The commentaries attributed to Confucius on his work on the I Ching are designed to do just that. Commenting on *K'un* (yin), he described it as being in harmony with the boundless, embracing and illuminating everything. He says it is in tune with the nature of the Earth and is the force through which individuals find success.

Today we are encouraged to think that success is achieved through ambition and effort of will, but Confucius said that going with the flow, being in tune with the planet on which we live, is the vital ingredient for true success. Yin is associated with the 'feminine' principles of nurturing, preservation and attunement – hence the association with Mother Earth.

Balancing this, in his commentaries on *Ch'ien* (yang), Confucius said that this force works through change and transformation. Everything finds its nature and destiny through this natural process, which encompasses the more 'masculine' principles of strength, movement and commencement. Of course, this does not limit men or women to just one of these forces; we all need both, but to different degrees. In fact, wherever there is yin there is also yang, and vice versa.

This concept that all life and all energy is composed of these two balancing forces was developed in an age when the spiritual emphasis was upon finding personal enlightenment before you could be considered ready to give others the help they really needed. Going within was the most important thing you could do. In these days of the new age, the emphasis has changed. Now that the stability – and even continuance – of the world is threatened by the existence of nuclear weaponry and potentially disastrous pollution, there is no longer the luxury of waiting until you are fully enlightened before you start to help the planet spiritually. Everyone can do something; everyone can heal; everyone can pray; everyone has some knowledge to share. You still need to go within, of course, because the outer life can ultimately only be a reflection of what is happening on the inside, but you do it as and when you can. Karma is such that you will find the space you need to do this, providing you take it.

To help you prepare yourself to be a healer, which is an ongoing process, here are seven exercises, divided into three yins, three yangs, and one combined exercise. Each of the yins has a balancing counterpart in one of the yangs. The first yin of calm, for example, is an inner state, whereas the first yang of charisma is an outer expression. The second pair, meditation and prayer, are the highest forms of mystical practice at an inner and outer level respectively. Visualization, the third yin, can manifest outwardly as a positive attitude, the third yang. Finally, there is a simple breathing exercise to balance the energy of each force. These seven can be applied in different degrees to different people at different times, so pick and choose which of them you need to work on most at any given moment.

Three Yins

Calm

Stress has become, for some, the mental equivalent of poverty and deprivation in our super-materialistic Western world. When increasing numbers have sufficient wealth to live a life of comfort and comparative luxury, they are also developing stress-related conditions in unprecedented numbers. The International Labour Organization revealed in 2001 that about 10 per cent of workers in the UK, US, Finland and Germany suffer from stress, anxiety and depression. At a purely financial level, the cost of stress to the British economy (in terms of sick pay, lost production and National Health Service expenditure) has been between £5 billion and £7 billion a year.

Another poll conducted by MORI in November 2000 showed that 78 per cent of workers say that they have experienced health problems as a result of stress at some time. Other reports have shown that children as young as primary school age are experiencing unacceptable levels of stress.

The link between mind and body was illustrated in a report released by the University of North Carolina in May 2000, which detailed links between heart attacks and anger. It concluded that a person who is prone to anger is three times more likely to have a heart attack or sudden cardiac death than someone who is not. This finding was especially true of middle-aged men and women. The results, which were based on people with normal blood pressure, confirmed that emotional states such as anger, anxiety and depression are likely to have a detrimental effect on health. Researchers analysed data from 13,000 people over a six-year period, 256 of whom had heart attacks.

Some psychologists identify four keys to managing anger: not misinterpreting other people's behaviour to you as hostile; identifying factors in your upbringing which predispose you to anger; learning ways to express legitimate anger; and forgiving those who hurt you. It is interesting to see psychologists, tackling these issues from a purely health angle, coming to some of the same conclusions as religious doctrines have for centuries from a moral perspective. These four points really boil down to: understanding others; self-knowledge; self-control; forgiveness. Sound familiar?

Stress is not necessarily a bad thing; it is uncontrolled stress that can be damaging. There is no proven link between physical comfort and inner peace, despite the massive advertising industry which constantly tells us otherwise. Of course financial deficiency is often a cause for unhappiness (though not always), but it is far from clear that the opposite is true – that financial wealth leads to happiness. As celebrity after celebrity reveals – or has forcibly revealed by the media – details of their unsatisfactory lives, it becomes clear that wealth and fame are not the things they were cracked up to be.

Peace and happiness are experienced in a stress-controlled but not necessarily a stress-free environment. They are essentially to do with the inner life, not its reflection in the outer world.

Of course we have to get all this in perspective. In some ways, stress is self-perpetuating. If you believe you are suffering from stress, then you will become more stressed, and so it feeds off itself. Even old-fashioned things like worry and conscience are regarded as stressful, and if we eliminated them altogether we would be living in a totally amoral, self-centred world in which the only thing that concerned us was removing all distractions from our own peace and quiet.

There are precedents for this in history. The Empress Catherine the Great of Russia was protected from the truth about the suffering of her subjects to the point where she was led to believe they were living in some pastoral, idyllic world. This was fine until she had to travel somewhere and pass the wastelands of deprivation, which characterized whole tracts of Tsarist Russia in the 18th century. Her advisors went to tremendous lengths to avoid her discovering the truth, even painting scenery on massive canvases so that as she passed she would not see the shameful reality. Admittedly this was not just to reduce her stress levels, but also to protect her advisors and court from the repercussions of her finding out how false their information was. But it does show that some stress can be necessary and beneficial. If people did not feel upset and therefore stressed by the suffering in deprived parts of the world, they would not be inspired to do anything about it.

Another far more significant example of this was the Lord Buddha. So saintly was he that his father, a local king, went to tremendous lengths to make sure that he should not witness any suffering in the kingdom. When he did by accident one day, he set out on his journey of self-enlightenment, which resulted in one of the most effective practical philosophies ever for discovering peace and wisdom within. It was the 'stress' of seeing the awfulness of pain, poverty and old age which motivated the Lord Buddha to give up his kingdom, wealth and family. This stressful experience ultimately led to his enlightenment, and that of many others.

We have to determine the stress which is illuminating and the stress we should be eliminating.

So, how do you control your stress levels and eliminate unnecessary stress? Professor Charles Figley[2] tackled this problem under acute conditions when he co-ordinated post-traumatic care of the survivors of the 1995 Oklahoma bombing. Among the so-called 'power therapies' which he identifies as being helpful was one called Thought Field Therapy (TFT). This is a system devised by a psychiatrist called Roger Callahan, in which the patient assesses their levels of distress – anger, fear, numbness, grief, etc. – on a scale of 0 to 10. They then used the principles of acupressure or shiatsu to reduce tension, after which they reassessed themselves. When the level reached 1 or 0, the process was complete.

This process of self-assessment reminds me of the Buddhist concept of 'mindfulness', in which you detach from your thoughts and emotions simply by watching them. This is really a basic form of meditation, which is one of the most effective keys to illuminating and eliminating stress.

Meditation

'The point of philosophy is to start with something so simple as to seem not worth stating, and to end with something so paradoxical that no one will believe it.' These words were written by the British philosopher Bertrand Russell in 1935 with some irony, proving that many an untrue word is spoken in jest. They are, in fact, the exact opposite of the truth. The point of philosophy is to perceive the nature of apparently contradictory and complex forces as a simple reality. This cannot be done with the intellect alone – even with one as distinguished as Russell's – it is predominantly a result of intuitive realization.

Western philosophy, with its roots in ancient Greece, is the product of brilliant, penetrating, but often convoluted logic; Eastern philosophy is built on a direct awareness achieved primarily through the meditative process. In fact, nothing could be more simple than the fundamental purpose of meditation: to observe the mind and, in doing so, to become one with that part of you which is beyond mind – the real or divine self.

The very fact that you can observe the mind proves that you must be more than mind. But writing it like that makes it just an intellectual theory; experiencing it through meditation makes it a living reality.

The meditative process is broken down into various stages, depending on how close you are able to come to your real self. Different teachers use different terminologies, but all are agreed that there are three levels, which in Sanskrit are called *dharana* (concentration), *dhyana* (meditation), and *samadhi*. Dr King calls them concentration, contemplation and meditation. His concept of meditation was far more advanced than the colloquial use of the word nowadays.

Even within these levels there are many different stages – the 20th-century yogi Sivananda, for example, describes several different degrees of samadhi.

Despite these many levels of attainment, the benefits of meditation are usually immediate. I have taught hundreds of people around the world the principles of meditation, and have been amazed that nearly all of them experienced a state of peace within literally the first few minutes.

All you have to do is be seated with the spine straight, but as relaxed as possible; breathe as deeply and evenly as possible, and start to watch your thoughts. This can be difficult at first, because the mind is programmed to jump constantly from thought to thought and attach to each one in turn. Meditation is a process of detachment through observation – instead of thinking about something, you allow the thoughts to go where they will. With patience and persistence, this will start to happen and you will move into a different state of consciousness, in which the brain waves are emitted at a slower rate. This induces a state of greater tranquillity and depth of perception, but less mental activity.

Experimentation into the different frequencies of brain-wave emission has been conducted extensively by scientists using a piece of apparatus called an electroencephalograph (EEG). Using the Greek alphabet, they refer to four brain-wave states – though it looks as though whoever initiated this programme did not know the alphabet very well, because the letters come in the wrong order.

The first are Beta waves, which come at a rate of between 13 and 28 per second, when we are in our normal state of active, conscious thinking.

The second are Alpha waves, which come at a rate of about 10 per second, when we start to enter a state of contemplation or mild meditation.

The third are Theta waves, at about three to six per second, when we are dreaming or in a deep state of meditation.

The fourth are Delta waves, at below three per second, which are associated with deep sleep.

Many people inhabit the Beta wave state until they go to bed at night, and then mysteriously enter the Delta wave state when they go to sleep at night. The next thing they know is that the alarm has gone off and they are back into Beta again. Meditation enables you to experience the profoundly significant states of perception in between these two, which are arguably the most valuable of all.

Of course, you do not have to practise a system of meditation to do this. Poets like Wordsworth and Tennyson, for example, describe entering sublime states of consciousness, which were obviously deeper than the normal Beta state of mental activity, and many people just hit upon them through mystical, artistic or contemplative events occurring in their lives.

For a healer, it is certainly very beneficial to spend some time in a contemplative or meditative practice, because it will help to bring an inner state of peace which you can then radiate to those you heal. They will pick up on the vibration you radiate. Meditation also enables you to switch your inner calm on and off at will. There are times you want to be peaceful, and times when you need to be dynamic and outgoing, but you need, as a healer, to be able to induce both states of consciousness – the yin and the yang.

Meditation for Calm

- Sit on a hard-backed chair or, if you practise Hatha Yoga, adopt an asana such as padma, or just be seated on the floor cross-legged. The important thing is that your spine is straight, and you are not tense.

- Breathe as deeply and evenly as you can without any strain.

- Now start to distance yourself from your thought processes. See your brain, not as the root of all consciousness, but rather like a radio receiver. Your thoughts are the radio waves flowing through the receiver (brain), which is not tuned to any particular frequency but just responds to whatever signals it receives in a haphazard fashion.

- Your key word is ALLOW. Allow whatever thoughts that come, be they in words, images, sounds, smells or just moods and feelings, to wash over you – to pass through your brain and onwards. If you have never done this before it may feel a little strange at first, but with practice you will get the hang of it. You should start to feel a sense of peace, relief even, as you just let go.

- Remain alert and focused, but not in an active mental way so much as an observational way. You are moving your mindset into a different mode. This is easier for some than for others, depending what your occupation in life is.

- If you find your brain jumping from thing to thing like a grasshopper, you are starting to get it. Don't try and stop this happening, just ALLOW the thoughts to go where they will, even if you do not like them much. After all, you are not your thoughts – you are more than your mind, or you would not be able to watch it.

Some people find it difficult to get started on a practice like this. They feel they need something specific to focus on. The things we do focus on in life, though necessary, are often consumed in petty detail and lead to a sense of frustration. There are intense pressures upon people nowadays, but the creative nature within us is often starved. The remedy for this is visualization.

Visualization

In May 2000, MIND, which is the largest mental health charity covering England and Wales, published the results of a survey of 550 people who suffered from mental health problems, including depression, anxiety, phobias and schizophrenia. You may be surprised to learn that as many as one in four of us will suffer from a mind-related problem at some time in our lives.[3] I interviewed a representative of MIND at the time for a piece I was writing for *The Observer* on alternative approaches to mental health. She told me that they had been surprised by the consistency of the results from this survey. Apart from dietary findings, such as a link between bananas and improved mood, there were some more unusual findings. Three-quarters were affected by the seasons, most finding their states of mind deteriorating in the winter months. The most commonly dreaded event was Christmas (49 per cent), followed by deaths and funerals (19 per cent). But the most significant finding to me was the extremely beneficial effect of participating in creative activities: 39 per cent cited listening to music; 25 per cent gardening; 24 per cent writing; and 21 per cent painting. Colour was also considered important, with blue having the most positive effect and black the least.

The curative effects of creativity derive from the use of the right hemisphere of the brain – which governs our imaginative, intuitive functions. The left hemisphere of the brain – which governs deductive, rational functions – is overused in today's world to the detriment of the right. Both are essential, but the former tends to be neglected in favour of the latter in our educational, legal and political systems and the general culture of the modern world.

Attempting to restore the balance between these two has been the focus for a number of personal development workshops and holistic therapies. One of the latter, called Eye Movement De-sensitization and Reprocessing (EMDR), was developed for the treatment of trauma. The patient is asked to focus on the trauma and at the same time silently follow the fingers of the therapist with their eyes. This causes the two hemispheres to link up, bringing a mental balance and relief from the trauma. Some counsellors have described it as more effective than conventional therapies because it quickly helps clients to bring feelings and memories to the surface and then deal with them.

Visualization is a vital tool for the healer. At first, you will need to use your imagination as a creative faculty to invoke the spiritual energy you need to heal with. Gradually, it will no longer be imagination at all. Because the energy really does exist in abundance throughout the universe, you will tap into it, feel it, and possibly see it. But visualization is the key to making this possible.

You can do this at any time, not just when a patient comes to you for treatment: you see a sick person walking outside your house, or an animal in pain by the roadside, or a plant withering in a flower bed. Obviously, the first thing you would do is to make sure they are getting whatever physical treatment they need – perhaps the plant needs watering! But, as well as this, you can use the power of your visualization to immediately send them white light. This can make all the difference.

Visualization of White Light

- **Stand with your hands by your sides, palms flat against your thighs.**

- Breathe as deeply and evenly as possible, without any strain.

- Now imagine a shaft of white light coming down from above your head and through and around your body and aura. You are virtually enclosed in a pillar of vibrant, scintillating light through you and several inches around you. It is so bright that you feel it would dazzle the vision of anyone who looked at you now.

- You may start to feel a tingling sensation, which is the effect of the universal life-forces coming into contact with your aura and psychic centres. You are being literally 'charged up' with spiritual energy, just as a battery is charged with electrical energy.

- This is the energy you need to practise healing. Because white contains all the colours of the spectrum, you will attract whichever colours you need to your aura, but at this stage just visualize white.

- If you have difficulty in 'seeing' the white, use a physical object which is pure white, such as a blank piece of paper. Physically look at it, then try to remember the colour and take it into your visualization. Memory can aid visualization, just as visualization practice will improve your memory.

Three Yangs

Charisma

Charisma is not always thought of as a good thing, because it has so often been misused. The charismatic salesman, politician or preacher who convinces you of something which is not really true, just by force of personality, is understandably shunned. In a spiritual context, however, charisma is a wonderful thing which can inspire, uplift and encourage everyone you meet. It is just another word for personal magnetism, which is very misunderstood. We often have stereotyped concepts of a magnetic personality, thinking it must be extrovert and outgoing, like that of an actor who can never switch off. The secret of charisma is not to change your personality, but to project it. If you have achieved an inner calm, your charisma will radiate it outwards. Charisma is expression; it is all about sharing your positive qualities with others; at its peak, it is an outpouring of light; in its very essence, it is giving.

A healer is a radiator of light, and as such must possess personal magnetism, even though at a higher level than most people are used to. This is because the energy from a healer is radiating through higher chakras as well as lower ones. The usual idea of a 'magnetic personality' is related to the lower three psychic centres: the base, sex, and solar plexus centres. Sexual magnetism is the most popular kind, and the most financially marketable. It is the key ingredient of celebrity status, or what is often called star quality. It is easy to recognize and respond to for most people, and yet it is not the most powerful. The solar plexus radiates tremendous power of a dynamic, stirring, more mental kind, and this too can be felt from some leaders, statesmen and authority figures. But it is only when you reach the heart centre that love energy starts to be radiated in its pure form and, because this can be subtler, it is not always detected so easily. Yet it is far more life-changing for those who come into contact with it.

By and large, impressed as you might be by their dynamic presence, you are not likely to be healed or have a vision of your life's purpose just by coming into contact with most celebrities. You might even be disappointed and wish you had never met them. But in the presence of an advanced spiritual personality who radiates energy through their higher chakras as well as their lower ones, you can be changed for the better by their very presence.

You can become such a charismatic presence yourself. People may not be aware consciously of the energy you radiate, but wherever you go you will change the atmosphere for the better. You will become a healing presence wherever you go. Using the lessons of the Yin cycle, by purifying yourself and discovering a profound inner peace you become ready to then radiate an impersonal, constructive love energy wherever you go.

Sometimes this will be deliberate, when you consciously send energy to a specific source; sometimes it will be purely instinctive. It will just happen, because you have cleansed the channels through which the internal psychic energies flow, and they will radiate outwards from you wherever they are needed. It is something you must be able to switch on and off – you do not want to be completely drained by everyone you meet. But, on tap as it were, there is a reservoir of energy to augment your personality into a charismatic expression of love. It might be compassion, forgiveness, gentleness, strength or any other quality, but the free flow of energy through your chakras, especially the higher ones, will empower these very qualities. You will uplift and inspire, sometimes without saying much. You will be a comforting presence, a rock, on some occasions; an invigorator, even spiritually aggressive, on others. You will become a vehicle for spiritual energy, which is the most elevated form of charisma.

The next step is to channel the energy directly, through the practice of prayer.

Prayer

A poll conducted for *Newsweek* in 2000 showed that 84 per cent of adult Americans believe that God performs miracles, and that 48 per cent have experienced one. Three-quarters of American Catholics, 81 per cent of Evangelicals, 54 per cent of other Protestants and 43 per cent of non-Christians and people of no faith say they have prayed to God or a saint for a miracle. The idea that prayer is an outmoded or unusual practice is bunkum. Most of us do it at some time in our adult lives, and many of us regularly.

The Vatican and at least one Islamic group have instituted procedures to discover whether reported healings are beyond medical explanation. Such studies have already been done. In 1988, Dr Randolph Byrd, a prominent cardiologist, conducted a study into the effects of prayer on coronary patients. A computer assigned 393 patients at San Francisco General Hospital either to a group that was prayed for or a group that was not. The prayer groups were given patients' first names and a description of their medical problems, and prayed each day until their discharge. After 10 months it was established that the prayed-for patients were 5 times less likely to require antibiotics, 2.5 times less likely to suffer congestive heart failure, and less prone to cardiac arrest. Coincidence? I don't think so.

An analysis in the US of 42 scientific studies examining 126,000 people indicated that churchgoers, which also included those attending synagogues, mosques and Buddhist temples, are 29 per cent more likely to live to an old age. Is it that they value life more highly and therefore look after themselves better, or is spirituality really good for you anyway? An exercise in Nottinghamshire in Britain in 2000 indicates the latter. Local Churches were invited by police to pray to reduce crime in the area, and achieved significant results. There was a clear drop in crime, particularly among the young.

Such exercises have been commonplace in other parts of the world such as Tibet and other parts of Asia and Africa, but not in the 'civilized' West. The Aetherius Society, of which I am Executive Secretary for Europe, has had considerable results from a spiritual mission called Operation Prayer Power. In this mission, spiritual energy has been stored in physical containers called Batteries. As controversial as this may sound, it is the result of a branch of science called radionics, which combines gold, crystal and other substances which attract and retain the natural flow of psychic energies. Once stored, this prayer energy can be released to specific locations at specific times to help relieve catastrophic situations. This has been done on many occasions with fantastic effect. I know this may sound far-fetched, but please check it out with The Aetherius Society (see the Appendix).

You can pray, and you can get fantastic results from your prayers, which I will develop more fully in Chapter 8, but in the mean time here are some basic, non-denominational principles you can follow.

How to Pray

- **Prayer is simply the radiation of spiritual energy through the person praying to a specific source. This may be a higher being which does not actually require your energy but for which you feel great reverence, such as the Virgin Mary, Sri Krishna, the Mother Earth or the Sun.**

- **In order to pray you need to be unobstructed, particularly at the palms of the hands and the heart centre, so that the love energy can flow freely through these chakras. Visualize white light travelling through you to the source of your prayer.**

- **The choice of prayer is up to you, but it should be in all ways constructive and not aim to control others, only to help and heal them.**

- **Above all, make sure that your prayers are always completely positive.**

A Positive Attitude

There is an abundance of proof that positive thinking really works. In 2000, researchers at the Mayo Clinic in Minnesota released the results of a long-term study into the relationship between people's state of mind and their longevity. A sample group of 839 people were interviewed between 1962 and 1965 and classified according to how optimistic or pessimistic they were. Thirty years later, the same group was surveyed again and it was discovered that optimists had a 19 per cent longer and healthier life on average. Dr Toshihiko Maruta, a Mayo Clinic psychiatrist, was quoted in the press as saying, 'The survey tells us that mind and body are linked and that attitude has an impact on the final outcome, death.' This was taken as evidence that positive thinking leads to a longer and healthier life.

After reading the report, Professor Martin Seligman[4] called for programmes for pessimistic people to change their thinking and so lower their risk of physical illness and death. In other words, he advocated that positive thinking be formally incorporated into medical treatments.

This is borne out by the so-called 'placebo effect', which behavioural psychologist Paul Martin[5] defines as 'a palpable demonstration of how our psychological expectations can override the signals coming from our body'. The word *placebo* originates from the Latin word for 'I will please'. A placebo is an item of medication (the classic case being a sugar pill) which is given to patients who believe that it has healing properties when it has none whatsoever. It works purely through the patients' belief that it will work.

There is also, incidentally, a 'nocebo effect', where harmless substances believed by individuals to be harmful have led to various illnesses.

Nowadays, placebos are often used in so-called double-blind trials by pharmaceutical companies, in which patients do not know whether they have taken a real medication or a placebo. Statistics have been thrown up in the air by the success of placebos in curing patients. Double-blind trials have reported improvement in anything between 25 and 75 per cent of patients, showing the power of a positive, optimistic attitude. This is particularly true of ailments with a clear body-mind link, such as chronic pain, hypertension, angina, depression, ulcers, asthma, arthritis and migraine. Some claim the positive effects of placebos on more serious complaints including heart disease and cancer. They appear to do more than relieve pain, affecting stress levels, lowering blood pressure, reducing hyperacidity and, some say, even aiding in the shrinking of a tumour.

Leading researcher Howard Brody[6] has called placebos the 'body's inner pharmacy', which seems to be a very accurate description. One strong theory is that certain endorphins are released within the body by the patient's belief in their recovery, which combat pain and achieve more joyful states of consciousness. A new area of medicine called psychoneuroimmunology (PNI) is being developed to utilize the mind–body connection.

Professor Herbert Benson[7] identifies three elements in the placebo response: the patient's belief, the physician or healer's belief, and a belief that comes from the two. A positive approach by the healer and patient can make a big difference in healing, as in other forms of treatment. Faith by the patient is not crucial, but it can help. In methods of Faith Healing, the patients have to have a religious belief in either the treatment or the healer before they can be healed at all. This is a limiting form of treatment. It can work, but can also fade with the patient's faith, perhaps after a high-octane evangelical or other event is over.

Healing has a strong basis for success with or without the element of faith. In fact, patients do not even have to believe that it will work. But there is no doubt that a positive attitude on the part of both healer and patient can make all the difference.

There is always a balance to be struck in positive thinking. This is well expressed in the philosophy of two contrasting Stoic philosophers from Rome some 2,000 years ago. The first, Epictetus, observed that 'people are disturbed not by things but by the views which they take of them.' A positive attitude to things – looking on the bright side of life (but without the Monty Pythonesque irony) – will tend to make those very things better. Seneca, on the other hand, as already mentioned advocated pessimism so that you would never be disappointed. If I had to choose one, it would definitely be Epictetus, but Seneca is right about unfulfilled expectations being a bitter pill to swallow.

My Stoic advice is: always be optimistic about events over which you have full control; where other people or situations are involved, be prepared for the worst; if in doubt, be optimistic. In the case of your own health, for example, always adopt a positive attitude; in the matter of a relationship, on the other hand, be positive but also accept that there is another person involved who may not behave exactly as you want them to.

It is really all a question of setting the right goals and then going out positively to achieve them.

Another balance to be struck is that between truthful self-knowledge and total confidence in yourself. This is difficult to get right. Self-esteem is valued, but egotism is frowned upon. What is the real difference between these two? Self-delusion. An egotist cannot see their faults, while someone with high self-esteem is aware of their strengths. The most important thing is self-honesty.

We have limitless potential – divine potential, according to yoga philosophy – so we have every reason to have high self-esteem. But we have much to learn, and by definition many failings to improve upon, so humility is called for. The trick is to get the right balance between these two extremes, and always to be honest about them.

It is a good exercise to review oneself in an honest light, warts and all, and then immediately afterwards to focus on one's inner potential and what one can and will become. You can feed yourself the mental food of a positive suggestion such as:

I AM LIMITLESS.

I AM DIVINE.

I WILL CREATE PERFECTION.

I WILL SUCCEED.

You can encourage yourself just as surely as you encourage others, and this will radiate a contagious sense of confidence – not a confidence born of an overweening and deluded ego, but of honest self-appraisal and determination to manifest your glorious potential. Be absolutely sure of this potential, because it is there, just waiting to be tapped.

A Yin–Yang Breathing Exercise to Bring in Balance

Just as the ancient Chinese divided life into two complementary forces, so too did the yogis of India and Tibet. As an individual develops, psychic energies within them flow through tiny channels on each side of the spinal cord. On the left is the channel called *ida*, and on the right, one called *pingala*. In the middle is a channel called *susumna*, with an even smaller one within it reputed to be a hundredth of the width of a hair, called *citrini*.

The yogis taught that different qualities could be cultivated by drawing the energy through one channel at a time. Through *ida* flow the energies associated with yin: calmness, peace, and inner reflection. Through *pingala* flow the energies associated with yang: dynamic expression, practical manifestation, and charisma.

The following exercise will balance the yin and yang energies within. It is based on the concept that the in-breath (literally 'inspirata') and out-breath should be equalized – the former could be associated with yin, and the latter with yang.

- Sit upright, with your chest, neck and head held in a straight line. Do not hunch up your shoulders. Keep your spine straight and the rest of your body relaxed at the same time.

- Breathe in slowly and steadily through both nostrils for a count which is within your capacity.

- Breathe out for the same count, thereby making the inhalation the same length as the exhalation.

- After a little practice, the in- and out-breaths will automatically equal each other. When this stage has been reached, you can then add the following mental affirmation, which should flow in and out without any strain of any kind:

I AM NOW PURIFYING MY MIND AND BODY.

There are many other ways you can purify yourself to become a powerful channel for healing, using spiritual development methods. But there is no need to delay your healing work while you do so. This can continue alongside your practice of healing. If we all waited until we were ready to become healers – or spiritual teachers, for that matter – the work would never get done. We would all be far too busy working on ourselves. So, whatever stage you are at, providing you have the desire to give healing, you can do so. In fact, those who think they are not ready may well be more prepared than those who think they are.

Like learning to swim, sooner or later you have to take the plunge. All the theory in the world, and all the practice in a shallow pool, will not fully prepare you for the deep waters. So it is now my privilege to initiate you into the most effective method of healing I know: the *King Technique*.

5 The King Technique

This book is not only the product of my experiences, but more importantly Dr King's, since I have been allowed by his executors to publish his very powerful method of healing, known as the *King Technique*. This has been used successfully to heal tens of thousands of people all over the world. I have used it myself, and have taught hundreds of others to do so. I have seen brand new healers get superb results on conditions ranging from a minor headache to partial blindness. Hip conditions, rheumatism, arthritis, severe stress, back pains, gout, depression, asthma, muscular contractions, convulsive spasms, traumatic shock, whiplash, toothache, migraine, heart conditions, HIV and cancer are just some of the conditions which have been assisted or completely cured by healers using the *King Technique*. And this by people who, for the most part, did not know they could be healers until they used this technique. It is tried and tested: it works.

Because I recommend the *King Technique* above all others, it forms the centrepiece of this book. It was devised by Dr King in the late 1950s, and has been used by thousands of healers since then with a very high success rate. The vast majority of patients who are treated at an Aetherius Society Centre with this technique, for example, tell us that they have improved as a result. Some just feel better and are more prepared to cope with their illness; some are partially (though not completely) healed; others are totally healed in what appears to be a miraculous fashion.

Of course, you should never guarantee that a patient will be healed, or give false hope: many will be healed, but some, sadly, will not.

Healers can be people of all types, but they all have the same burning desire to help others. Applying this technique with love and compassion has brought successful results, which have astounded some of them. Here are just half a dozen cases, selected at random.

Healing Results

This is not an attempt to provide scientific evidence for healing, but to pass on a few anecdotal experiences I have received from healers who use the *King Technique*.

> **A woman with a painful hip, who was reliant on using her walking stick, came for healing in London. After a few treatments, the pain was reduced so much that she could walk unaided and threw away her walking stick.**

> **A terminal patient in a hospice in Michigan, US, who suffered from advanced emphysema, was on oxygen 24 hours a day, could not get up on her own and was in a permanent state of bodily stress. The only relief she received was after receiving healing, to the extent that her attending physician gave written authorization for these treatments to continue.**

A man from Bristol had suffered a year of intense pain caused by a trapped nerve in the neck. Numerous trips to doctors and chiropractors, and drug treatment, had not brought him sufficient relief. After three treatments, he declared himself completely healed.

A woman had such severe back problems resulting from a childhood accident that she had been unable to sit or lie on her back for 20 years. After trying several medical methods, she turned to a healer, who had come to Britain from Ghana. She had to stand throughout the treatment, but after just one treatment she could be driven home seated, instead of lying down on her front, for the first time in 20 years. After three further treatments she was completely cured.

A man from Toronto, Canada was scheduled to undergo surgery to remove a large portion of his colon. He received three treatments prior to the scheduled surgery date, and when he went to hospital it was discovered that he no longer needed surgery.

One heart-warming case from Nigeria concerns a healer of just 11 years of age. She performed healing on one of her classmates, who had a severe headache, during a school break. Before the treatment was finished, the patient was laughing because her headache had completely disappeared. The budding healer was given a new school nickname: 'Doctor'!

These are just six of hundreds of reports made by people from around the world who use the *King Technique*. But, there is one definitive way to check just how effective this technique is, and that is to use it regularly yourself. It is not the only healing method that works, by any means, but it is the most comprehensive I know. It is a perfect blend of ancient yoga philosophy and modern spiritual practice.

What it Takes

In this chapter I will quote extensively from Dr King's own description of his technique. As in Chapter 3, his writings will be in italics to differentiate them from my commentary and further explanation.

In raw nature, the strong take from the weak; but in the science of healing, the weak take from the strong. If you are spiritually weak, then you cannot give spiritual energies to another who may be suffering and is spiritually stronger than yourself. So therefore, you must prepare yourself as a channel for a flow of these natural forces through you. The more spiritual your outlook, the better the power will flow and the purer it will be. Do not forget that the healing power is coming through your aura, subtle nervous system, physical nervous system and body, so it will be coloured by you. Therefore, you as the healer should be as clean in thought and deed as is possible for you.

These are high standards, which should not put you off but inspire you to higher and higher levels of attainment. Of course, if we all waited until we were completely spiritually pure, there would be hardly a healer on Earth – I, for one, would not qualify. But being a healer can become a 24-hour activity – everything we think and do will affect, to some degree, no matter how small, our powers as healers. It can become what used to be described as a 'calling', though even as I write this it occurs to me that many are called, but few are listening.

Eat the right foods, without making a fetish of it; drink the right liquids, again without making it a fad; and breathe in the right way; pray in the right way; have the right outlook; have a balanced faith in your own ability; and then you are able to take an important step towards your success in this spiritual science.

I must stress that this is the ideal, not the minimum qualification. Everyone can heal; these are ways of making the healing powers flow more freely and potently through you. And that pretty well sums it up, except for one final word: before you start treating patients through the laying on of hands, you would be well advised to find out your legal and insurance position regarding healing. There may be certain legal requirements and responsibilities laid down in your area, which you need to adhere to. In Great Britain there are organizations like the Institute of Complementary Medicine, of which I am an Advisor, which provides detailed information about legality, insurance and so on. This is not the place for the legal and bureaucratic niceties of different countries and states regarding contact healing. But it would be advisable to check yours out before you start to give treatments, especially to the public.

The Mirror Test

We can all heal, but here is a way you can monitor and check your healing performance. I have tested this on dozens of people, including highly sceptical journalists who were nevertheless open-minded enough to give it a fair chance. Some of them were amazed by the results they got.

Even without any clairvoyant powers at all, you can test the strength of force of your natural magnetic output which acts as a carrier-wave for the more subtle blends of forces which make up the whole of your potential as a healer. The only real way for the average person to test the quality of their healing power is to give healing. But the pressure of your magnetic power can be very simply tested in the following way.

1   **Stand about 2 feet [60 cm] away from a large mirror in which you can plainly see the upper part of your body – face and head. The cleaner the mirror is, and strangely enough the better the quality of the reflective surface, the better this test will work for you. Put your feet together, stand straight and extend your right arm in front of you with the palm of your hand a few inches from the mirror. The fingers should be spread apart and held up vertically.**

2   Visualize healing energy as a white light coming down from above the head, through yourself and out from the palm of the hand. At the same time, try to feel what is happening to the hand.

3   When you can physically feel a slight tingling sensation on the tops of your fingers and a very slight warmth over the palm of your hand, then very slowly move your hand away from the mirror until you arrive at a spot where you are no longer aware of these sensations.

4   Try the same test with the left hand.

5   Try the same test again, but this time with both hands extended in front of you, palms facing the mirror, and move both hands away until you no longer feel the impingement of forces which cause a tingling in your fingers. They are your own forces being reflected by the mirror back into your hands again. If you are powerful enough to take several steps back from the mirror in order to get out of the area of impingement, then your natural magnetic power is good.

6   If you are able to solicit help to further the scope of this experiment, get someone to measure the distance between the palms of your hands and the surface of the mirror with a tape measure. Make a note of the distance with great care. Any time in the future, you can make the same test upon yourself and you can see whether the distance decreases or increases. If the distance decreases, it means you are out of tune and need some exercises to revitalize you. If the distance increases, then it means that the pressure behind your natural magnetic flow is becoming better and better. Even three or four inches will signify considerable improvement. As you give more and more healing, you will find that this distance will increase.

In the beginning, if you can honestly feel the impingement on the tips of your fingers and a slight warmth in the palms of both hands up to a distance of 20 or 22 inches [50–55 cm], then your magnetic flow is above average, probably enhanced by prayer or other spiritual practices you have been doing. A good healer can easily increase this distance, especially at certain times of the day and year, to several feet.

You are now ready to start on your treatments, but first there is some very simple apparatus you will need.

Healing Apparatus

All you really need in the way of physical equipment is a white cotton coat, which must always be kept spotless; a bowl in which to wash your hands before and after every healing; and a stool upon which to sit your patient, if possible, kept only for this purpose; and a quiet place with subdued lighting. If you want to use coloured lighting, then green is the best. Gather these few essentials together and you can start using my technique, which does not require any psychic abilities whatsoever in the beginning or the ability to make a diagnosis.

The reason healers often wear a white coat is not because they are frustrated hospital doctors, but for a sound metaphysical purpose. When giving healing you come into contact with the psychic contamination in the auras of your patients. As described earlier, this manifests as a form of discolouration of one kind or another. If you were to wear coloured clothing, it is possible that the colours in your clothes would attract the colours in the aura of your patient and thereby contaminate your own. By wearing white, you neutralize this effect because no particular colour is attracted to you.

Cotton is recommended because it is not a good conductor of psychic energies. Strange as that may sound, in the science of radionics certain materials, such as gold, crystal and, in the case of garments, silk, are known to be more psychically conductive than others. As with the colour white, the use of cotton will protect you from attracting contaminated energies from the aura of your patient through your clothing and into your own aura. It is this kind of attention to detail which marks out the *King Technique* from every other I have come across.

The water bowl should be non-metallic so as not to attract or retain psychic energy, as you will see, and should be placed nearby, together with a clean towel. I have personally met an excellent healer who never washed her hands after a treatment and developed arthritis in her fingers. It might be dismissed as coincidence, but there is no doubt that a healer is coming into contact through their hands with the psychic sickness of the patient. Frequently washing the hands in clean, cold water will ensure that you do not retain any of this within yourself.

The final piece of apparatus, the stool, should be wooden if possible, because wood will not retain the psychic energies of the patient as much as plastic or, particularly, metal will. Just to cap it, paint your wooden stool white if you can, and reserve it purely for healing use. As with the coat and bowl, you would ideally keep it separately in a cupboard or somewhere apart from day-to-day activities. This is not only a protective measure; it will also start to imbue these items with a healing vibration so that, when they are used, they immediately tend to create the atmosphere and environment you want. If you cannot obtain a wooden stool, then a plain wooden chair will have to be used, but the patient will need to sit sideways upon it, so that the healer can work on their front and back.

The place you heal will depend very much on how much space you have available, and where people wish to receive healing. I have attended festivals of many kinds all over the world, and given healing with sometimes dozens of others to scores of patients between us. There have been instantaneous and sometimes miraculous healing results, even though the atmosphere is not always ideal. But you just have to get on and perform your treatments regardless. In an ideal world, you would be able to set up your own centre, reserved for nothing other than healing and spiritual practices. You could light it dimly with a green bulb, use incense or aromatherapy oils to create a conducive perfume, and put on music that will soothe and relax your patients before and between treatments. These are two extremes – you will have to adapt your situation accordingly. If you are able to have a space reserved for your healing, it will build up an atmosphere which will become a healing zone – as soon as people step into it, they will already start to feel better.

Performing the Technique

Step One: The Practice of the Presence

The first step in the *King Technique* is a most beautiful practice called The Practice of the Presence. I have been performing it regularly for 30 years and regard it as one of the most spiritual exercises I have ever learned. It can be as important as food and drink – sometimes more. It cleanses the aura from all kinds of mental and even physical pollution, which you may have encountered along the way, often through no fault of your own but because of the vibrations you have had to absorb from places and people. If you don't believe me, travel regularly on the London Underground!

In the Practice of the Presence you will use visualization to invoke three energies: white light, which represents the universal life-forces flowing throughout the universe; a golden sphere, which represents your higher self and your unlimited potential; and the Violet Flame, which is a real, protective and transmuting power associated with Mother Earth.

This mystical practice should be thoroughly learned, practised and used before your healing session begins and at the end of your healing session, because it will, as well as raising your consciousness, help to clean any contamination from your own aura which has been picked up from your treatment of the patient. If you do the Violet Flame part correctly, you will become so impregnated with this power that you can transmute conditions, which you have taken from your patient, by the application of the main healing technique.

1   Stand up with spine straight, head held erect and your arms down by the sides with the palms flat against the outside of each leg.

2   Close your eyes and make the following visualizations. Think a vibrating, pulsating white light down through your brain. Feel the whole of your brain vibrating with this dynamic, magnetic charge.

3   When you really experience that feeling, then visualize a golden sphere just above the top of your head and request with open-minded belief that the golden ray of spiritual energy impregnates your mental, physical and auric bodies right down to the heart centre.

4   Finally, think up the transmuting Violet Flame through your feet and legs, and throughout your physical and auric bodies. Bring together the three great powers in the heart centre and visualize them as moving upwards, right above the top of the head into the golden sphere. Hold this visualization for a minute or two and then, depending on your religious beliefs, say a prayer of thankfulness to God for these cleansing and protective powers.

Treat this Practice with the utmost reverence, for as you practise it, it will become more and more powerful within you, to such an extent that you will feel the effect it has on your healing.

Step Two: Seating the Patient

Before starting, the healer should wash his or her hands very thoroughly in hot water and finish up with a good rinse in tepid water. In fact, hand-washing facilities should be close at hand, as healers must wash their hands in clear, cold water before going from one patient to another – hence the bowl. If you want to use coloured lighting in the room, then green bulbs are the best for healing, but do not have the lighting too subdued, since you will have to be able to see what you are doing! The room should be as quiet as possible. After invoking healing power by the use of deep breathing, prayer or mantra, you are ready to start healing.

These preliminary stages have already been covered in some detail, but are repeated because they are all essential. Sometimes you will feel charged up and ready to go, with very little preparation; on other occasions you will have to work hard to get yourself into the right state of consciousness to be a channel for healing power. You will find that, with practice, it will become more and more automatic. In fact, the times when you really do not feel like healing at all can be the most potent of all, as though the extra effort you have to make is a karmic manipulation to attract greater healing powers to and through you. Now you can seat the patient, as in illustration 2.

Sit the patient down [on a stool, or if one is not available on a short-backed wooden chair,] ... preferably facing East. The healer should remove all rings, bracelets and watches ... and request that the patient does likewise. If the patient wears glasses, request that these be removed as well.

... approach the patient and ask them in a quiet voice where the pain is. Wherever the pain is, the whole technique should be followed very closely, as described and illustrated, with particular concentration on the painful area.

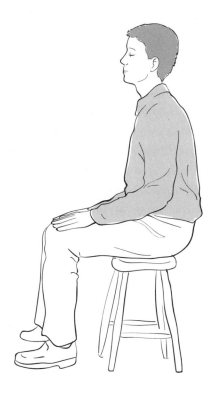

Illustration 2: The Seated Patient

... you should only talk to the patient during the Healing when it is absolutely necessary to do so, i.e. asking questions about their pain or general condition.

[as far as possible,] the patient should sit relaxed with eyes closed, with their hands on their legs, palms down and fingers spread slightly apart ... This tends to hold the Spiritual power in the body that you [will be putting into them].

Whenever you are invoking psychic energies, it is advisable to face East, because that is where the source of these universal life-forces rises every morning. They come through and from the sun and permeate the whole solar system, which is really comprised of solidified sunlight. Rings, bracelets and watches are removed since they have radionic properties and may attract and thereby stem the flow of the universal life-forces through the healer and patient. Glasses, too, can do this, particularly if they are metallic, as well as being an impediment to some of the healing passes the healer will need to perform.

Obviously, if a patient is not comfortable removing any of these items you will have to compromise, but really they should go out of their way to co-operate with the healing treatment and follow your request to adopt the posture described by Dr King, for very precise reasons. Although the *King Technique* does not require any kind of faith from the patient, the more they try to assist the healer in his or her work, the better for them. After all, you can only receive if you are willing to give – and the patient is about to receive energy from you.

The whole question of interaction between healer and patient will be dealt with in Chapter 7, but conversation during the technique should be kept to an absolute minimum so that you can concentrate fully on the task which is, quite literally, at hand.

Step Three: The Seven Passes

*After ascertaining where the painful area is from the patient themselves, and after you feel the power is flowing through you, then approach the patient in a definite, sure manner, so to give confidence to the patient that you know what you are doing. Make **seven passes** across the forehead of the patient and right down the back with your two hands close together, ending the pass at the base of the spine by throwing off any auric condition your hands may have picked up ... This movement should be light and yet fairly quick and sure at the same time. Always keep in mind that the positive centre in the middle of your right hand gives out energy, and the negative centre in the middle of your left hand tends to attract that energy given out by the right hand centre back to itself again. In other words, you are working with two subtle instruments; one which gives off Healing energy and the other which 'tends' to attract that Healing energy to itself, thereby causing a flow between the two psychic centres in the palm of each hand.*

With some women, this polarity is reversed, but you will gradually learn this from experience. Actually, it does not really matter whether it is a right–left polarity or a left–right polarity as, with this technique, being as complete as it is, the energy will still flow in the way that it is supposed to as you will discover.

This concept of polarity is absolutely vital to the technique. At first, you may have no idea whether your flow is right–left or left–right, in which case you should heal on a right–left basis unless or until you discover otherwise. With practice, maybe instantaneously, you will know in which direction the power is flowing. In some cases one of your hands or palms can become burning hot, which is an indication that this is your positive centre. A good pendulum dowser will be able to tell you, if you are not sure yourself. But the important thing in the early stages is to establish the principle that you are creating a circuit of power within yourself – you are virtually a polarized, magnetic battery.

*All the time you are making these **seven passes**, visualize yourself as filled with Healing energy and this energy going **into** the patient. **Visualize the Healing energy as a pure, white vibrant power.** Do not colour it in any way. It should be a white coloured energy and you should visualize it as such. Not blue, red, or any other colour ...*

*Each one of these **seven passes** should be performed in a continuous, smooth movement. Do not do these jerkily nor stop in the middle of the pass while you alter your position. With some practice you will be able to perform the passes firmly, quickly and surely ...*

These passes are most important because, if done correctly, they will:

A   **stimulate the nervous system of the patient and charge it with healing power**

B   **allow you to pull away adverse conditions from the aura of the patient.**

These dual functions permeate the *King Technique*, which is designed to both charge the patient's aura with positive psychic energy and remove contaminated psychic energy from their aura. If both these services are performed successfully by the healer, the patient will have a healthy aura, untarnished by the illnesses and imbalances they had. This must manifest through the levels, either immediately or in time, as an improvement in their physical health as well. Study illustrations 3–7 carefully to see how these passes should be performed.

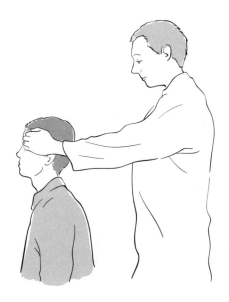

Illustration 3: The Healing Pass (i)

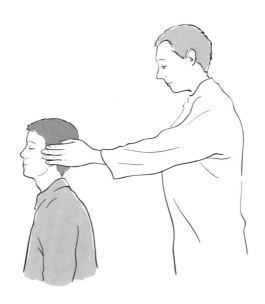

Illustration 4: The Healing Pass (ii)

the *magic* of healing

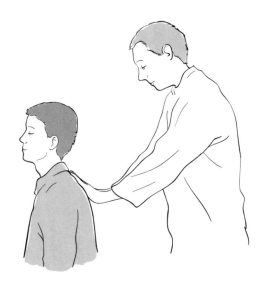

Illustration 5: The Healing Pass (iii)

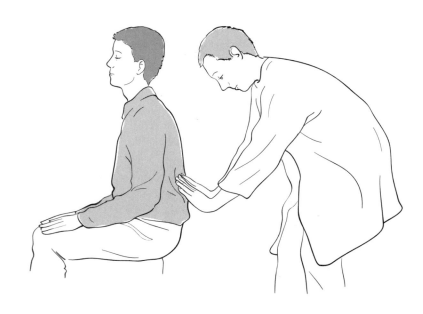

Illustration 6: The Healing Pass (iv)

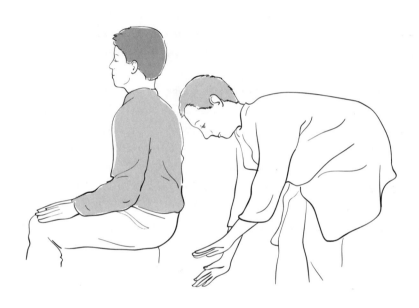

Illustration 7: The Healing Pass (v)

*You should start off with your hands flat against the patient's head as in illustrations 3 and 4. In the position shown in illustration 5 you will easily be able to keep your hands flat against the shoulders of the patient, but when you move further down the back, as in illustration 6, you will find it easier to move the **palms** of your hands away a little but you must keep firm pressure on the finger tips.*

*Each of these seven passes must have contact with the body of the patient **right down to the end of the spine** and only after the end of the spine has been passed should you move your hands away as in illustration 7.*

*... It is essential to keep your hands close together and then throw off any condition you pull away, by moving both hands **away** from the patient in the same direction. If you feel a cool clamminess on your fingers you will know that you have pulled away a condition and make sure that you shake this condition from your hands [as per illustration 7], which is only held by the light magnetic attraction of the psychic centres in the hands ... and can be shaken away easily, **if done immediately** ... make sure that you throw off any condition that you pick up from the patient. And make these passes in a determined and strictly disciplined manner, throwing off the adverse condition **in one spot of the room only**, making absolutely sure that it is not thrown back onto yourself again or that it is not thrown onto another patient who may be waiting!*

As you can see from Dr King's meticulous description, you are dealing with real substance. Even though it is psychic and you may not be able to feel or sense it initially, you must always remember that it does exist and has powerful properties. Hence the careful way Dr King devised this technique – I cannot think of another which is so detailed in its prescriptions regarding the psychic implications of healing.

*After some practice at this, some of you will actually **feel** the condition and be able to throw it off quite easily and also you will be able to 'see' this condition clairvoyantly as you throw it off.*

Some healers do this technique of the passes so well that they have to move one hand over the other to throw off the condition, just as they would if they were ridding their hands of soap suds or mud.

When you do this, try to do it behind the patient so as not to alarm or insult him in any way ... Treat your patient with understanding and compassion, in the same way that you ... would like to be treated.

In the early stages, if you do not feel the energy you are pulling away from the patient, keep your hands together throughout the pass. If later on you clairsentiently feel it or detect this energy through another of the psychic senses, you may need to be more flexible in your use of your hands to be sure you actually pick up all the discoloured energy you wish to remove.

Step Four: Charging the Psychic Centres

Having generally cleansed and charged the aura, you will now be working on the major chakras to bring overall balance. Healers who work only in the area of pain and do not include the seven major psychic centres are missing out on a crucial psychic balancing process. Just as physical pain can be rooted in an entirely different part of the anatomy from the one you feel it in, so the psychic nervous system depends on the balanced flow of energies throughout the aura, and particularly generated from and through the seven major chakras.

For example, a headache can be caused by lower back trouble, and gout pains in the foot may have their origins in a digestive and dietary disorder. In the same way, the aura should be regarded holistically. By bringing balance throughout these psychic centres, the whole aura will be affected in a most beneficial way. Being psychic in concept, this technique has the added advantage of working at a mental and emotional level, as well as a physical one. It is vital to remember that the psychic centres through which you are radiating healing power are located in the exact centre of your palms; you should be careful to position your hands so that your palms are centrally located over each chakra.

Illustration Number 8 shows the first psychic centre position.

*The next step is to stand to one side of the patient and then you should hold your right hand over the forehead and the left hand immediately opposite, over the back of the head, making sure to have palm contact throughout this procedure. As you do this, you should visualize a **white** [healing] power leaving the palm of the right hand and travelling through the head of the patient into your left hand. Visualize the whole of the brain of the patient being charged by this vibrant **white** light.*

*Hold this position for a minute or so and when you feel impressed, then move to the other side of the patient, reversing the hands, i.e. putting the left hand over the forehead and the right hand on the back of the head immediately opposite to it, and visualize the **white** light leaving the palm of the right hand and travelling through the head of the patient to your left hand. The better you do this, [and] the better your visualization is, the more success you will have from it.*

If you become certain that the psychic centre in your left palm is the positive, transmitting polarity, and the right is the negative, receiving polarity, you should reverse the order by starting with your left hand on the person's forehead and right hand behind their head first. It is better to put the positive charge at the front first. But, if in doubt, start with the right – even if this were to prove the 'wrong' way round, it would still work effectively.

You will notice that there is no direct attempt in this technique to charge the highest centre of all – the crown centre at the top of the head. This centre is regarded as too spiritual to be charged with the hands of a healer directly, but by placing the hands on the forehead you are situated

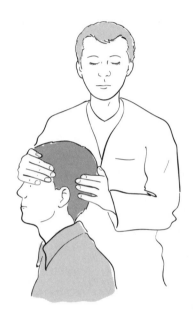

Illustration 8: Charging the Christ Centre

between the two centres in the head, and nearer to the third eye. Both these centres will benefit from this position, though you are not exactly on top of either for the very good reason that they are elevated seats of consciousness, which need to be treated delicately. The fact that they are grossly under-used by most of us does not in any way lessen their potential for total knowledge and spiritual oneness.

If you lose your visualization, keep your hands where they are and quickly say to yourself a Prayer, at the same time taking a few deep breaths in and out, which procedure should bring your concentration back to your visualization again.

*It is important to be able to hold the visualization of the **white** light travelling from one palm of the hand to the other through different parts of the body of the patient, as you will see when you proceed further with the technique. In the beginning you may have to correct yourself as your concentration wanders, but it is all a matter of experience which comes with self-discipline and practice. Students have found that Prayer is beneficial to them because it helps them invoke the Healing power in such a way that they can feel the power surge through them as they are giving a treatment and this also enhances their visualization at the same time. If you also perform some controlled breathing exercises such as inhaling the breath **slowly and silently** though both nostrils and exhaling it **slowly and silently**, you will find that your concentrative powers are immediately enhanced because on every breath that you breathe in you take in the Universal Life-Forces with the breath.*

Naturally you can perform another practice, providing it is of a high Spiritual nature, with which you may be familiar in order to control your concentration so that you can hold it throughout this technique where specified.

This is very personal. Some will favour silent prayer or a mantra to maintain their concentration and enhance their healing power, others will use breathing or another method. After a while you will be so aware of the power flowing, which may feel like an intense heat in the palms of your hands or some other sensation, that you will not need to invoke it constantly. Even so, you will need to remain vigilant and focused on the task at hand to ensure that the power does not diminish. It may come in waves or pulses, which you can time with the rhythm of your breathing.

The next step is to move your position again so that you can put your right hand over the throat of the patient and your left hand over the back of their neck, again visualizing the white Healing power travelling from the palm of the right hand through the neck into the left hand. Now, you can also move your visualization so that the white light also charges up the whole head of the patient, as you did in the beginning.

There is an emphasis throughout this technique on the energy rising upwards within the patient. This conforms absolutely with yoga teaching on spiritual advancement, in which the mystic forces are directed upwards through the nadic channels within the aura. As your hands move downwards through the different psychic centres, you will still be charging the higher parts of the body and aura of the patient as well as the centre you are in physical contact with.

Hold this position for a few minutes and then move to the other side of the patient and reverse the hands, again visualizing the flow from the right hand, which will now be at the back of the neck, into the left hand which will now be over the throat. And again, visualize this energy rising up and charging the whole head of the patient; ears, eyes and brain; so that the head is charged with this Spiritual power.

It is not necessary to visualize the aura of the patient. This technique is deliberately based on physical contact between your healing hands and the patient's body. Because there is an interrelationship between the psychic centres and the physical organs, there will be an automatic interchange of energy; you do not need to worry about visualizing this

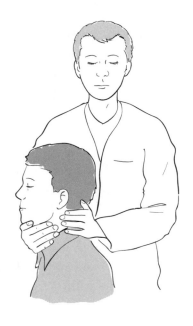

Illustration 9: Charging the Throat Centre

happening. As long as you charge the locations you are in contact with, the rest will happen automatically.

Some techniques attempt to lay the hands on the aura rather than the physical body. Although that can work, it is not so precise, because the size of different patients' auras can vary enormously, which means that with some you may be inside the aura and with others too far away. This can lead to a less definite contact, and therefore the charging of the body and aura of the patient can be diminished.

Next, move your hands down over the equivalent of the Heart Centre, which is not over the physical heart itself, by the way, but just about the beginning of the main chest bone, and your left hand opposite this in the back, again holding the visualization of the energy as a white light flowing from right to left, and this time, move it upwards by visualization and to the side, so that it impregnates the physical heart, nerves, blood, throat and head of the patient.

After holding that position for a few minutes, reverse the hands as you did with the Throat Centre.

Men will have to observe the required levels of propriety when treating ladies on this psychic centre. You will have to determine what is appropriate in this respect, but if necessary you will have to hold the hands away from the body.

Illustration 10: Charging the Heart Centre

the magic of healing

Illustration 11: Charging the Solar Plexus Centre

The next step is to put the right hand over the Solar Plexus region and the left hand on the back opposite the centre as shown in illustration 11. Use the same visualization, but this time try to visualize the power travelling upwards through the inside of the body, up through the neck and into the ears, eyes and brain of the patient. After a few minutes, reverse the hands and continue with the same visualization.

This is particularly important for those patients who lack energy or are over-stressed. The solar plexus is the battery centre and is the first area where depletion of energy levels is experienced. Even for those with excessive energy, charging this centre will bring a positive, balancing effect.

*This time come down slightly **below** the spleen area with the right hand, and the left hand as near to the base of the spine as possible. Visualize the energy running between the hands, as usual, but again this time, try to visualize it rising up through, not only the whole of the body, but also going up the spine to the head and curing all ailments as it does so. This is the most difficult visualization, really, because now you have to make your energy travel through the trunk of the body, which will need some practice before you can do it correctly. But again, practice makes perfect.*

After this, reverse the hands, putting the right hand as near to the base of the spine as possible, and the left hand in the front and a little lower down than the spleen, and adopt the same visualization.

For the reasons mentioned earlier, the spleen centre is used instead of the sex centre and this is, like the first chakra position, a combination of two centres. Again there is a continual flow of energy upwards throughout the trunk, neck and head and including all the organs of the body. Although the legs and feet appear to be neglected in Step Four, because of the psychic interaction throughout the aura there will be a flow of energy wherever it is most needed from these major psychic nerve centres. You are now ready to move to specific parts of the patient's anatomy which require healing.

Illustration 12: Charging the Spleen Centre

Step Five: Treating Specific Ailments

Now you have given a general Spiritual Healing treatment to the patient and after this you can concentrate on specific areas.

It is only after completing all the previous steps that you now start to concentrate on specific areas of discomfort.

[For the purpose of illustration,] let us assume [that], in your preliminary talk with the patient, you have been informed by them that they are suffering from a pain in the shoulder, making movement painful. You have already asked them if they have had X-rays for this [and you have ascertained that they are taking whatever medical treatment is appropriate for their condition, but they have come to you for additional help].

Move to the side of your patient as per illustration 13, putting the [palm of your right hand] on the front of the shoulder and the [palm of your left hand] on the shoulder blade behind it, and again visualize the white light travelling through the body of the patient from the right palm to the left palm. Do not send this energy anywhere else in the body as you did previously, but localize it in this one particular area.

After a few minutes, reverse the palms ... this time sending the energy from the right palm over the shoulder blades into the left palm over the front of the shoulder. Hold this position for a few minutes ...

The exact time you spend treating an individual area will depend in the severity of the patient's illness, how many specific areas you will be treating and how long you have got. It is not necessary to spend too long on an area; a few minutes on each side should be adequate. It will also depend on the reaction of the patient and just how receptive they are to your energy. After a while you will get a feeling about how long to spend, and will be able to judge accordingly.

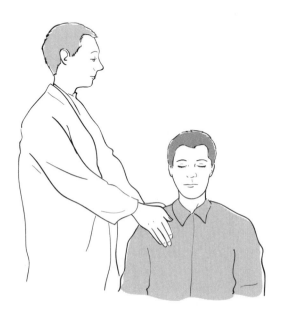

Illustration 13: Treating a Specific Ailment

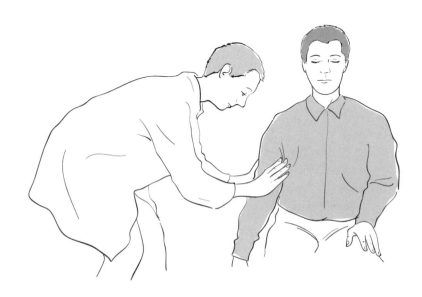

Illustration 14: Pass for Ailment (i)

the *magic* of healing

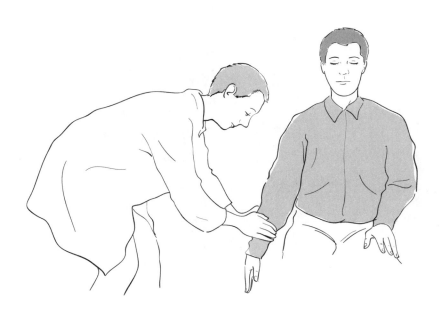

Illustration 15: Pass for Ailment (ii)

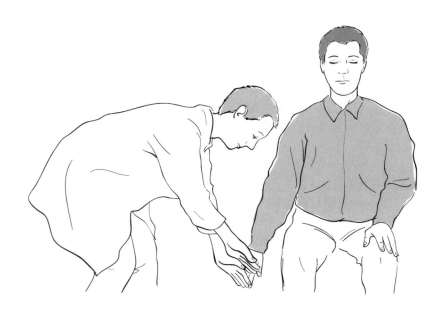

Illustration 16: Pass for Ailment (iii)

*... Ask the patient to hold out their arm and, with both [your] hands cupped around the arm, make some passes all the way down the arm, throwing off the condition as you did with the first passes (see illustration 14). Make sure that you throw the condition into the same place as you did the first item and in this way it will be localized for a short time anyway. Make these passes quite definitely. If you do these correctly, you should be able to throw off an adverse condition which **must** have its reflection in the aura of the patient, because of the fact that they are suffering from a pain in the shoulder. Do this with precision and self-discipline, believing in what you are doing, and you will find that it will work for you. Like all aspects of Spiritual Healing, the better you do these passes, the more sure will be the results.*

*Depending on the apparent severity of the condition are the number of passes. If the condition to you seems to be very severe, then do at least **21 passes** of this nature; if not so severe, then **14** should suffice (see illustrations 14, 15 and 16).*

Again, you will develop a feeling for how many passes to do; and it will depend on how much time you have, and how many areas the patient requires treatment in.

You will notice that the *King Technique* employs multiples of seven many times. As mentioned in Chapter 3, seven has long been regarded as the mystical number associated with wisdom, contemplation and spirituality. It is not by chance that there are seven major chakras in the aura, which makes it a highly significant number in yoga. It also appears frequently in Western writings, including the Bible, which often uses seven or its multiples, such as seventy-seven times seven, etc.

If the patient complains about any other centres of discomfort, you can adopt exactly the same procedure as you did with the shoulder and arm.

In the case of the solar plexus region, for instance, the passes would be made to the side, throwing off the condition in the same place as you threw off the condition in the first passes of the technique.

You will have to judge appropriate ways of performing the healing treatment, depending on the area you are healing. Always balance out the right–left charging process with its exact reverse, and then perform either 14 or 21 passes. These will need to be performed in such a way as to give you maximum opportunity for pulling off contaminated energy from the patient. You will need to make them lengthy, as with the shoulder where the passes continued down the full length of the arm. For example, a treatment of the ankle or foot may lead to passes being made down much of the leg. A treatment of the head may lead to passes being made from the head down the neck and even the spine, as in the original seven passes. This type of flowing movement gives you more opportunity to both charge the patient and remove as much as possible of their discoloured psychic energy.

Step Six: Smoothing the Aura

Stand near the patient with your hands above their head and making sure that the power is flowing through you as shown in illustration 17.

This step is all about feeling. You have given a dynamic injection of spiritual energy to your patient and removed discoloured energy from them in a positive and firm way. Now you need to allow the feeling of love for your patient to permeate you as you perform the closing elements of the technique.

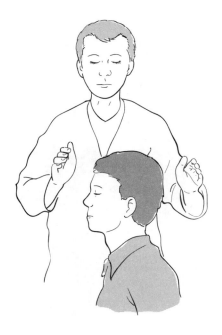

Illustration 17: Smoothing the Aura (i)

Illustration 18: Smoothing the Aura (ii)

the *magic* of healing

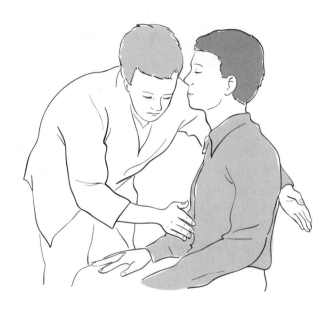

Illustration 19: Smoothing the Aura (iii)

Then move your hands **close** to the body of the patient, as shown in illustrations 18 and 19, all the way down right to the feet. In this way, you are putting the last charge into the aura of the patient. You must move your hands **all the way around** the patient, trying to visualize the vibrant white Spiritual Healing power leaving your hands and charging up their aura.

This is also done for another reason. With the Healing, you must have, to some extent, caused slight ... **'ruffles'** or **excess pools** of energy in certain parts of the aura of the patient, and these have to be smoothed out, and they can be if you try to visualize the aura while making sure that you pass your hands **all the way over as much of it as possible**.

The aura is normally between 3 and 5 inches (7.5–12.5 cm) away from the physical body, so you can use this as a yardstick in estimating where to pass your hands.

This is the one part of the technique in which you are giving healing without being in physical contact with the body. With practice, you should start to get an impression of where the hands should be with each individual patient, or you may even feel the aura itself.

Although you are still charging the aura of the patient, the emphasis is upon smoothing out any imbalances, which may have been caused by your healing, particularly in the areas where you performed passes. You will find this a most beautiful part of the technique when you get used to it, which generally induces a feeling of peacefulness within the patient.

Step Seven: Cleaning Up

After you have finished the treatment, the patient should be asked to leave the Healing [stool or] chair and then you should 'clear up the mess,' so to speak. You have pulled away conditions from the aura and from painful

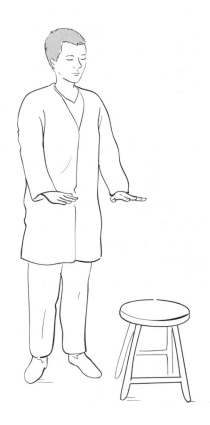

Illustration 20: Cleaning Up

parts of the patient, and the etheric matter is still laying there on the floor where you deposited it, so now you must transmute it.

Hold your hands above the position where you threw off the condition and practise the Violet Flame Practice ... You should visualize this Violet Flame as coming through the whole of your aura and thereby cleansing it for you, and also streaming from your hands and transmuting any adverse etheric condition which you threw off. While you are doing this, concentrate on the Healing chair or stool and send the Violet Flame over it and through it so that no condition from the last patient remains on or in this furniture.

The pool of contaminated energy, which you have placed in one position throughout the technique, now needs to be transmuted – and will be, by the wonderful energy of the Violet Flame. Just as seven is regarded as the most spiritual number, so violet is often regarded as the most spiritual colour, with the possible exception of gold. Violet has the particular properties of transmutation and protection, which makes it ideal for this purpose. It is a natural energy which comes from the Earth, so it should be visualized as coming up through the feet, legs, body and aura rather than from above, as with the white light, which travels through the sun and the cosmos as a whole.

For those who revere and respect the planet as a living, breathing goddess (known as *Gaia* in ancient Greece), a short prayer of thankfulness to Her can be said afterwards.

This is a practice you can use not just for healing, but at any time when you feel in need of protection and cleansing. The best way to do this, if it is practical to do so, is outdoors in bare feet. However it can be done very effectively anywhere – even on the top floor of a high building – by using the power of your visualization.

When you feel sure that you have cleared up the condition, then you should make certain that you wash your hands in cold water before you continue with the next patient.

*Do not even shake hands with your last patient, or naturally the next one, until you have washed your hands in cold water kept in a non-metallic basin, which should be somewhere in the vicinity **but not too near** to the actual Healing stool.*

A light wash of the hands is all that is necessary at this stage, as water will clear any subtle condition from your hands which may be remaining. After you have washed them, then dry your hands on a clean cotton towel which should be laundered regularly.

Then you are ready to bid goodbye to your last patient and go on to the next one if this is applicable.

*This washing of the hands in cold water after **every** Healing treatment is an essential part of the technique and a step which should not be forgotten by the healer.*

It is vital that you do not carry over any of the discoloured energy from one patient to the next – hence the emphasis on using the water in your bowl. This will cleanse and protect you and anyone or anything else you come into contact with from then onwards.

Psychic energy is not some theory or faint hope; it is a very definite reality, which is why Dr King included these precautions, which are so often neglected by other teachers. You may get away with it or you may not, but it is not worth taking any chances. In fact, if you are treating a serious condition and feel the need to wash your hands *during* a treatment as well as at the end, you should certainly do so.

*If you have finished Healing for the day, then wash your hands thoroughly in cold running water, ending up by running water for about a minute over the **insides** of both wrists ... This will cut off the power flow from you so that you will not waste your valuable Spiritual energy ...*

Then take off your Healing smock or white coat and hang it away in such a place where it will not get dirty or be contaminated by other clothes. If there is the slightest feeling in your mind that it may be contaminated by the conditions of your patients, then throw it into the washing machine ... [If you can,] have two or three of them so that you have spares while one, which has been in use, is being washed ...

These are the final steps in a perfectly balanced and truly magical technique, which I thoroughly recommend to you. The length of time spent on each treatment will depend on how long you think the patient needs before they have received enough, and how much time you have at your disposal. A broad guideline would be 15 to 25 minutes.

As you become proficient in this technique, you will find that your treatments improve. There is no limit to your potential as a healer; it is all a question of how far you want to take it. Here is a testimony from a grateful patient who benefitted from the *King Technique*:

A Testimony for the King Technique

'For four or five years, I suffered pain in both of my knees as a result of a sports injury. The discomfort would be felt in both knees if I had to stand more than a few minutes.

'I had heard about spiritual healing from my brother and finally decided to give it a try. The year was 1977. Whilst I was sceptical that spiritual healing would bring relief, it certainly was worth trying before the surgery that a medical doctor had recommended.

'During my first healing appointment at the Michigan Branch of The Aetherius Society, the healer treated only one knee and suggested that I come back one week later for treatment on the other knee. The next day, my treated knee was completely better. The untreated knee showed no improvement.

'I kept my second appointment and my other knee was treated for the first time. To my amazement, that knee was also completely better within a couple of days.

'I went for a few more spiritual healing treatments on my knees to help ensure that the healing would last. It has been over 20 years since I have experienced discomfort in my knees.'

Read on to find out ways of enhancing your healing abilities and advancing yourself in the process.

6 *Enhanced and Advanced Healing*

Once you have learned the *King Technique*, you can enhance your healing in many ways. The most direct way is to potentize the treatment by working with another healer, especially when you are treating a critical condition. This can also be a way for a new healer to learn, by initially assisting an experienced healer while at the same time contributing to the treatment.

Healing in Pairs

Drawing on the concept of polarity, which is fundamental to the *King Technique*, it is generally most effective for the two healers to be of different genders (though this is by no means essential). A compatible man and woman working together are more likely to provide a balance of yin and yang energies, though you cannot dogmatically pigeon-hole either sex as exclusively 'yin' or 'yang'. There are also cases where two men or two women working together can be exceptionally effective, depending on who the healers are and the condition of the patient.

Either way, two healers working harmoniously together is bound to be more potent than one alone. In fact, it can be more than twice as potent because of the interaction of energies between the two, which can virtually create a reactive force within the aura of the patient.

This was well illustrated by one African couple who regularly healed together. One of their successes concerned a woman who was suffering from a blood clot on the brain, leading to almost total speech impairment and a lack of co-ordination in her hands and legs. An operation to remove the blood clot had caused a secondary clot to develop over her right eye, making it physically drop. After one treatment from this couple using the *King Technique* together, this woman amazed her husband and friends by being able to put on her jewellery unaided. After her second treatment, her doctor informed her that she had made 18 months' progress in a few weeks. After her third treatment, her speech was much clearer and she could do household chores, including cooking a meal for her family without help.

If you are performing the *King Technique* with a second healer, they should also have studied the technique so that they understand what is going on and how they can best co-operate with you. Like you, they should perform preparatory practices, especially the Practice of the Presence, before starting the treatment. They should wear a white cotton coat and remove all rings, bracelets and watches – for the same reasons as you – and they should wash their hands before and after the treatment.

From a purely mechanical point of view, during treatment they should be seated opposite the patient, directly facing them (see illustration 21). In this position they should not be an obstruction to you when you need to adopt different positions around the patient. If they do get in the way at all, you can simply ask them to move temporarily. Certainly you will be able to charge the major psychic centres as described in Step Four of the technique with your assistant in this position.

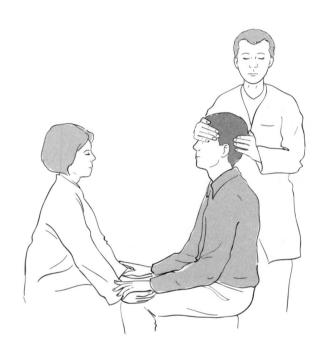

Illustration 21: Healing in Pairs

the *magic* of healing

The assistant should lay their hands upturned on the thighs of the patient, just above the knees, so that the patient's hands lay on top of the assistant's hands rather than directly on their own knees. The assistant's right hand will then be palm to palm with the patient's left, and their left with the patient's right. This brings a magnetic balance, allowing the energies to flow in a harmonious way throughout the patient. In this case, though, the helper should visualize their energy not going from right to left, but from both palms through the palms of the patient and throughout all parts of the patient's body and aura. The power of their visualization will be absolutely crucial to the enhancement of the treatment the healer is giving.

Sometimes healers can choose to work in pairs as a general rule, and can develop a strong healing relationship with another healer to the point where they take it in turns to heal or assist. This can depend on who is in the more dynamic state at the time, and on the condition of the patient. Experience can show that some healers are particularly good with certain ailments, others with others. This may sound strange, but I have met healers who specialize in, for example, eye ailments.

Sometimes healers working in pairs are so compatible that they can change places (healer and assistant) over the course of a single treatment. This can be done in a silent, unspoken way. Generally, though, it is better not to change over during any of the individual steps of the technique – for example, one healer should do all the seven passes, one the charging of the psychic centres, etc. One place where you may choose to swap, though, would be the treatment of the specific ailment.

Very good candidates for assisting with healing can be ex-patients who have themselves been cured. They want to put something back by helping others, and they can be the most effective of all because they know from firsthand experience that it works.

Your choice of assistant is vital, because the wrong assistant (someone who really isn't as motivated as you are, for example) can detract from the treatment. You could find that instead of them helping with the healing, they are actually drawing even more of your energy from you – in this case using the patient as a go-between! Far-fetched as this may sound, it has happened. Generally, though, an assistant who understands the technique you are using will greatly potentize the treatment.

But what if you need healing yourself and there is no healer available? The answer, then, is to administer healing to yourself.

A Technique for Self-Healing

'Physician, heal thyself!' Easier said than done. It is also highly questionable to imply that if you cannot heal yourself then you cannot heal anyone else. For one thing, it is easier to be motivated for others, sometimes, than it is for yourself. Just as you might put more effort into cooking for others than you do when you are eating alone, so you might find it easier to make an effort to heal others than yourself. The energy you radiate to a patient can be purer than when you heal yourself, because it is less tied to your own personal emotions. This is why it can be easier to heal a complete stranger than a loved one or relative with whom you have some type of emotional relationship. The very emotions can cause a dissipation of the energy, which should be the product of a pure form of love created by controlling the emotions. Most obviously of all, the very fact that you need healing at all indicates that your energy levels are not at their most potent, and therefore you are perhaps not in the best position to give healing at all.

But these are negatives, and the essence of healing is a resounding positive. I found the technique very effective myself when I was a student suffering from severe hay fever. Combined with homoeopathy, self-healing greatly improved my condition.

You can heal yourself, and there is no reason at all why you should not spend the energy on doing so, just as much as you do on healing anyone else. After all, the healthier you are, the more you are able to heal others.

As an extension of the *King Technique*, Dr King devised the following simple method you can use to heal yourself. Again, I will use italics to distinguish his writings from my own.

Step One: The Practice of the Presence

Start your self-treatment by standing up, facing east and performing the mystical 'Practice of the Presence'.

Follow the exact procedures laid down in Chapter 5. If you are not fit enough to stand, you can perform this practice seated on a chair, or even in bed.

Step Two: Energizing Yourself

*... lie down full length on a comfortable couch or your bed, in a quiet room away from traffic and fumes ... Then lay the right hand, palm downwards, over the solar plexus region. Lay the left hand, palm downwards, **on top of the right hand**. This will tend to enhance the flow of Healing energy through the nerve centres, especially concentrating it in the solar plexus region which is a very important battery for the human body. Then breathe deeply in a measured count, holding the breath for half the time of the inhalation and breathing out for the same count as the inhalation. The rhythm should be: 2-in, 1-hold, and 2-out.*

In *Pranayama* exercises, counts are often given to achieve different purposes. When the in-breath is as evenly matched as possible with the out-breath, a certain stability of energy is achieved within the psyche of the individual. This also ensures that the lungs are thoroughly cleared before the next in-breath, which means that far more air (and, therefore, universal life-force) can be drawn into you. An experienced instructor will not dictate the exact length of these in- and out-breaths, because each student varies in their capacity. The guideline is to make the breaths as deep as possible without any strain.

While you are breathing in, visualize the prana flowing into the body with the in-breath. While you are holding the breath, which must be done without imposing any strain on you, visualize the prana as a brilliant white light filling your body from head to toe. While you are breathing out, visualize the toxic materials leaving your body with the out-breath. **Do not put any other colour on the breath, only a brilliant white.**

It is important on the out-breath not to visualize negative energy leaving you and imbuing the atmosphere around you. There should be more of a sense of being cleansed. The toxic materials should have been transmuted by the white light, and therefore leave you enveloped in this light. Just as positive energies transmitted outwards will affect the whole environment around you, so must negative ones. Hence the need to feel cleansed of these toxic substances, but not to inflict them on the universal sea of mind around you.

After you have done this for approximately a dozen breaths, then continue with the same breathing rhythm, but this time, while you are breathing in, whisper to yourself 'Great peace, great peace.' Try to feel your whole body becoming relaxed and filled with deep, harmonious, relaxing peace.

You cannot create peace in the world as a whole, if you are incapable of finding it within yourself. Sooner or later the outer is always a reflection of the inner. This sense of inner peace has to be cultivated, particularly if you lead a stressful life. It will not just come to you uninvited; you have to allow it to come from the innermost part of your being. Just as you want to generate the calm and charisma you have attained within yourself for your patients, so it is necessary to first invoke a peaceful presence within you, before giving yourself healing. There is no need to force it, just let it happen and it will. The soul is crying out for us to sometimes stop and allow the superconscious aspect to take over. This is accompanied, at least initially, by a sense of deep peace. Later it might become a more active, inspirational energy, but the feeling of peace is a sure sign you are starting to go within.

Step Three: Charging the Psychic Centres

When you are relaxed, remain in the same lying position without moving, with the right hand palm downwards over the solar plexus region and the left hand laying lightly, palm downwards, upon the back of the right hand as previously stated. This will tend to lock the energy flow in the body and also charge up one of the main basic nerve batteries of the body, namely the Solar Plexus Centre.

When you feel a peaceful condition within your whole body, then placing your left hand over the Solar Plexus Centre and while continuing with a deep in and out breath, hold your right hand over your forehead.

This self-healing technique now follows the same principles as laid down in the *King Technique*. Just as a patient needs first to have an overall auric balance induced by charging up the main psychic centres in their aura, so too do you.

Visualize the pranic Healing power flowing from the psychic centre in the palm of the right hand down through your body to the Solar Plexus Centre where your left hand is. After a few minutes, move the right hand down and lay it over the throat, making sure that the centre of your palm contacts the front of your throat. *Then, move it down to the Heart Centre, the same position as you learned in the technique of Healing others. Now move the right hand and lay it over the Spleen Centre. Then*

*move the right hand on the solar plexus region and duplicate the whole
process with your left hand. You will not easily be able to hold either hand
over the base of the spine or the back, but frontal treatments should bring
good results, providing your visualization is as good as it should be.*

This approximates as closely to the *King Technique* as possible at an
individual level. When positioning the palms, allow the energy to flow
and it will do so. Because it can be more difficult to heal yourself, you
may need to make an extra effort to distance yourself emotionally from
the process by just letting it happen, as it were. Of course your positive
visualization of white light is as important as ever, but just let the energy
flow rather than trying to force it. The polarity principle remains with the
energy flowing right–left (assuming that is your positive–negative
alignment) in each position.

*... with the tips of the fingers of both hands, gently brush as much of the
body as you can reach, starting from the top of the head, down the face,
etc. with the tips of your fingers, while thinking to yourself that Healing
power is entering you and making you fit and well. Do this brushing at
least 21 times.*

This is a method devised specially for the self-healing process, because of its
gentleness and stimulating effects. You will find it extremely pleasant and
beneficial to apply to yourself. You are not in a position to perform definite
and sweeping passes on yourself, but this action will have a very beneficial
effect on the whole of your aura. Since it is so gentle, it is deliberately
positioned after the charging of the psychic centres, whereas the seven
passes used on other patients as part of the *King Technique* come first.

Step Four: Treating Specific Ailments

*Now, let us suppose your pain is in the left shoulder, then put the **left hand**
on the solar plexus and give treatment into the shoulder with the right*

hand as you would in the main Healing technique. If the pain is in the right shoulder, then reverse the position of the hands.

If the pain is in the legs or knees, you may have to sit up on the bed to give Healing to these spots. If you do, then lay the right hand over the front of the painful part of the leg and the left hand on the back of it for a few minutes, and then reverse the hands.

Try always to hold the visualization of being filled with vibrant, white Healing power which is driving the condition of discomfort from you.

The solar plexus centre forms the core of this self-healing technique, in that it is used as the balance for each position you adopt, with the other palm on the upper half of your body. The nadic linkages which run throughout the aura, causing an interconnection between major and minor chakras, is so perfect that this battery centre will be able to create a link with the energy flow from the other palm. In these cases it is not necessary or practicable to reverse the palms afterwards. However, in treating the legs or feet, this can be done – providing you can attain a comfortable position for the palms on each side of the affected area.

Step Five: Total Relaxation

*After you have done this, then lie flat again and take the measured, slow in, hold, slow out breaths without any strain whatsoever. It is up to you to work out for yourself what suits you best in this respect, but the rhythm of 2-1-2 should be adhered to. Then relax the whole body. I know that this is far easier said than done, but a few tips from the ancient science of Yoga should help you to do this. Lay the hands alongside the legs and ... **tighten up every muscle in the body as hard as you possibly can!** Really use effort in doing this, and then slowly – ever so slowly – relieve this tension until you have no tension whatsoever in the body. At first you may have to do this tightening exercise at least three times before you can obtain the* *desired results. But as one who has practised Yoga diligently for many years, I know that sooner or later this technique will help bring on a condition of deep relaxation.*

This may seem a surprising approach to relaxation, but I can vouch from personal experience that it really works. The process of tensing first enables the relaxation afterwards to be far more complete. During the tightening of muscles throughout the body, including even the facial muscles, you become aware of the tensions that were already there, and then, when you relax, these tensions disappear along with the ones you have just induced. In doing this exercise you will need to adopt a rigid posture and a grimace in the face, but disregard how you might appear – you are alone, anyway. You can go through the body bit by bit, particularly in the early stages, to achieve this thorough tightening. Gradually, it will become easier and easier to do.

Then relax completely.

*Starting from your feet, relax them. If there is any tension there, move them slightly. Try to get the tension out of the feet and gradually, mentally work all the way up the body, part by part, internal organ by internal organ, and relax it – until you are **completely relaxed**.*

This is a peaceful and joyful practice if it is done correctly. It will immediately induce a sense of self-healing, because in addition to the physical relaxation you will have induced, the psychic energies will be able to flow much more freely through you.

[To make this even more effective,] when you get to the heart, think first of all a great love for your own heart. You will, after some time, feel a response from your heart; then gently, delicately, with great love, feeling and compassion, ask your heart to relax, but to beat slowly and strongly. This will help to bring about a relaxation throughout the whole body ... Continue this until you are completely relaxed.

It has been stated by Yogi Masters that 15 minutes of complete relaxation done in the right way is equal to five or six hours of normal sleep, and I would agree with their findings ...

Complete relaxation is extremely rare, even during sleep. Hence the emphasis, particularly in Hatha Yoga, on exercises designed to induce total relaxation. Through doing these exercises you will be able to bring about deeper and deeper states of relaxation at will, which will help both in controlling stress levels and improving your sleep patterns. These, in turn, must bring about better health.

You will discover that the first time or two you try to relax it will be difficult, for all manner of thoughts will enter your mind. But gradually as you practise more and more, then you will become more and more proficient at it. It is in this deep relaxation that the Healing power which you have put into yourself will have a chance to bring harmony and ease where dis-harmony and dis-ease were making themselves painfully known.

It is not so much that disparate thoughts will suddenly start to enter your consciousness when you do this; it is that you are becoming far more aware of them. By relaxing, you tend to observe the mind rather than focus it on any particular issue. In doing so, you get a glimpse of all the myriad thoughts that are already floating through your brain, which is the first step towards controlling them.

Step Six: Cleansing the Area

After 15 or 20 minutes of relaxation like this after your self-Healing, then slowly bring yourself to activity. In other words, do not suddenly leap off the bed, but slowly bring yourself back to normal activity again, arise form the bed and perform the Practice of the Presence with special emphasis upon the Violet Flame part of this mystical practice. When you feel the Violet Flame rising through you, then wave your hands over the bed, as you

have been taught, to burn up any etheric condition taken off you ... in such
a way as to ensure that the whole bed and the room in close proximity is
thoroughly cleansed. Then, say a Prayer of thankfulness to God for the
Healing which you have given to yourself.

It will, of course, depend on your beliefs whether it is appropriate for you
to say a prayer. If you do believe in such things, you are giving thanks to
the universal source of all creation for supplying you with the energy
with which you have healed yourself. This has nothing whatsoever to do
with faith healing, because the treatment depends upon your efforts in
visualizing and projecting the energy, not on what your religious beliefs
are. It does, however, provide a beautiful balance to the practice.

Step Seven: Detaching from Results

And then comes one of the most important aspects of any Healing
technique, be it self-Healing or Healing another – a secret known only to
the few, though it is absurdly simple ...

This mystical key can be explained in one word – detach!

Ancient yoga philosophy constantly emphasizes the importance of
detachment. For example, mystics from East and West alike would have
been encouraged at one time to forego money. If your only goal were to seek
your own enlightenment, that might well be a means to an end. But in an
era of selfless service, money can be a very valuable energy in achieving
powerful results for others as well as yourself. What is required, in all forms
of energy and expression, is self-control. In healing, though, and particularly
self-healing, detachment at the end of the technique is an invaluable tool
in bringing about a magical effect from the healing technique you have
just used.

*When you have given yourself the Healing treatment to the best of your ability, taking as much care as you would if Healing a loved one, and after you have cleaned up the bed and room afterwards, then **detach** from your Healing – and the results! Do not give it a further position in your thoughts. In other words, have complete faith in your own abilities, in the technique and most important, in the fact that because you requested in a reverent manner the Healing power to flow, **know** that it did flow through you. That is why detachment is so important. It is the last link in the chain. It is as though you had complete faith and were expressing this through your detachment.*

Only attach yourself to your own self-Healing or the Healing of another when you want to perform it the next time.

This act of detachment is virtually an act of magic – by letting go, you are making a mental statement that you believe in what you have just done far more than if you were to hold on to it. This concept is inherent in the old Chinese saying: 'If you love something, throw it to the wind. If it is blown back it is yours for ever.' It is particularly important in the self-healing technique, because you are living with the ailment you are trying to heal, and therefore it is that much more difficult to detach yourself from it. It would only be human to wonder whether the treatment will be effective or not, but this very wondering is casting a mental doubt into the ethers, which will reduce the impact of the treatment.

This kind of detachment is also particularly important if you are working on someone who is emotionally close to you, when you are bound to have more personal expectations invested. This is why healers who do not know their patients are often better than those who do. But with the tool of detachment after the treatment, you can bring this under your control. It is simple, like so many powerful magical practices, but undoubtedly a very subtle way of enhancing your healing. So, it's a case of 'physician, heal thyself' – and then detach!

... ALL healers, whether they are in the best of health or whether they need a treatment or not can benefit themselves by this simple self-Healing technique ... the better you can perform this technique for your own benefit, the better you will be able to give Healing to others.

The beauty of self-healing is that, while you are healing yourself, you are at the same time enhancing your healing abilities. What a perfect way to get better! Whenever you give healing to yourself or others, you are simultaneously evolving.

One of the results of this is that you will start to get intuitive impressions in the process. This is not essential to the *King Technique*, but as you advance in your healing ability it may naturally start to happen. The secret is to ensure that you are getting genuine impressions, and not just imaginary flights of consciousness.

Getting the Right Impressions

One of the wonders of human nature is the unique combination of qualities that each of us manifests through the mysterious force of personality. This is never truer than in the area of psychic ability. I would caution, though, against passing any information on to a patient which may be interpreted as a diagnosis. You should not give anything which could be described as a medical diagnosis, since this is something that needs to be treated professionally and may well be subject to legal strictures. Even though you are not attempting to give a medical diagnosis as such, make sure no claims can be made later that you were. If in doubt, use the information you gain from your impressions for your personal guidance only, and do not pass it on to the patient. Some people, when told they may have an ailment they were not aware of, build it up and exaggerate it in their mind until, before you know it, you have supposedly told them they might have a chronic or even critical illness!

However, there are many cases where intuitive impressions can be very helpful in healing. This is just one, reported to me by a healer originally from Italy who used the *King Technique*. Her patient had hit his neck and back of the head on the metal surface of a door. He had experienced headaches for three months, and an area near his right ear was so painful that he could not touch it. After one treatment, the headache went and the pain in the patient's ear decreased, so he continued with further sessions. During the third treatment, the healer received an impression that something was wrong with the patient's left leg. She asked her patient, who informed her that he had vein problems, so the healer treated that as well, and the pain completely disappeared in that area as well.

You need to be 'in touch with yourself', as the jargon goes, to identify how you can best express your powers of intuition in a reliable and positive manner. Let's take a look at some of the ways you can do this.

Physically

You may pick up the physical ailments of your patient as a physical sensation in your own body. You may get a minor reflection of their pain in your own anatomy, so if it is in their left shoulder, for example, you'd actually feel, usually to a lesser degree than they, a definite pain in your left shoulder. This kind of 'sympathetic' reaction is well known between people who are very close to each other – for example between a husband and wife during the wife's pregnancy.

As a healer you will become more sensitive to everyone you meet, and you may find you get a pain in the throat or head when a friend of yours comes to see you with a sore throat or headache. It is a very direct, internal feeling, which requires careful discrimination. The imagination can run riot, especially in the early stages, and you must be careful not to jump to conclusions as a result of any physical sensations you are experiencing. It may just be that you have adopted a physical position you are not used to and your body is feeling it – this is nothing whatsoever to do with a patient.

I would advise you against making rash assumptions based on your physical feelings. If a particular sensation recurs when you are with a particular patient, you could certainly ask them if they have experienced any pain in that area. If the answer is 'yes', memorize the type of sensation you've experienced so that you can tell the difference, in future, between a genuine sympathetic reaction and an imagined one.

Mentally

Sometimes when you are giving healing, thoughts may pop into your mind as if from nowhere. Because you have attuned yourself to channel healing energies, you have opened yourself up to receive energy on a mental level, too. Words, images and occasionally symbols can float into your brain as though they carry some meaning for you.

First of all, you have to make sure it is not your wandering imagination. If there is a definite message for you to detect, it will not evaporate as soon as it comes, but hang around, as it were. It may be the thought pattern of the patient you are picking up, or it might be an intuitive impression from your own superconscious mind. In the latter case it could be sent to you by a guiding force, which I will explain later on in this chapter. In some ways, it does not matter whether it is from your own superconscious or from a higher source, because both will be worth listening to and taking note of. It will be some type of guidance to help you administer your treatment more effectively.

If it comes from the patient, you will be able to tell that it is related to their condition. It will be information designed to help you understand their condition and how to help them more. You should never try to use this ability to eavesdrop upon their innermost thoughts, and in fact you will not be able to do this. You will find that the information which comes to you from them is purely there to help you with their healing. For example, they may know at a subconscious level more about their ailment than they are prepared consciously to admit to themselves. The subconscious is a brilliant aspect of mind, which knows far better than the conscious mind how our bodies are functioning. Sometimes, by tuning straight in to this part of the mind at an intuitive level, you will learn more than you are being told verbally by the patient. As always, discriminate carefully, do not jump to conclusions, and be careful of what you pass on to the patient, especially if you are not sure yourself. Above all, do not get distracted from the task at hand: to give healing to your patient.

Emotionally

Health is so related to emotional make-up that this type of impression can be exceptionally revealing. Always remember that the information is being given to you to help you as a healer, not to give you information about the patient's private emotional life, which is really none of your business unless the patient wants to make it so. If you pick up, for example, that the patient is nervous, depressed, excited, lovesick or disappointed, it may help you to understand the reasons behind their physical problem. Additionally, an illness, especially a serious one, can affect a person's emotional state. They may suffer from anxiety or frustration brought on by their physical state. All this can affect the way you treat them. If they are very highly strung, you may decide to administer the technique in a gentle, soothing manner predominantly; if they are despondent and downbeat, you may want to perform more dynamic passes at the beginning, and so on. Do not pry, but a simple question before healing them, such as 'Are you feeling worried by anything at present?' might enable them to get a lot off their chest, which can then leave them more open to your treatment.

Psychically

These are specific psychic abilities which may start to develop naturally within you as you give healing. An inner psychic frustration, which you may not even know you had, will leave you if you give regular healing and open up the door to your latent psychic potential. However, before you can really develop psychically you must first be able to concentrate. Only then can contemplative abilities, such as psychic powers, be safely used.

Of the five senses, I have left out taste, since it is very rare in a healing context, but anything is possible and if you find you are able to gain impressions about your patients through psychic taste, then pursue it. It is a mark of the infinite variety of psychic expressions that there are so many ways of manifesting our natural spiritual attributes.

Using psychic powers to help the health and well-being of others is exactly as things should be, and any faith healers who say otherwise are motivated by a mixture of dogma and fear, which has no place in the healing process.

You will experience a beautiful sense of freedom when you start to use your psychic abilities to help others in one of the following ways. I must stress again, though, that this applies mainly to before or after a treatment, not during one, when you should be concentrating on the healing power flowing through you.

Touch

Psychic touch is the most obvious psychic attribute for a healer to develop, because of the direct contact you have with patients. You may start to feel different sensations as you place your hands on different parts of a patient's body. The first thing you are likely to feel is heat in the palms (and possibly the fingers) of your hands, which is a result of the universal life-forces flowing through you and causing some friction with the patient's aura. You may start to feel the contaminated parts of a patient's aura as a clammy type of feeling, tinged with what I can only describe as a distasteful feeling. You may also feel benign energies within a patient's aura. I and others who gave healing to Dr King, for example, at the end of his life would frequently feel very positive energies coming from him, even when he was in poor health. When these sensations are new to you, it may take a while to discriminate which is which, but after a while you will be able to sense what you are touching. This can help you to assess the state of your patient's aura and the quality of energy you are channelling into it.

The best-known method of psychic touch is psychometry, in which the psychometrist will hold an object and assess from this the vibrations it has been in contact with in the past. This can either be a ring, watch or necklace belonging to someone, in which case the psychometrist will learn about them, or something connected with a particular period of history or antiquity. Although as a healer you are not taking psychic touch this far, the patient's body and aura can become virtually 'articles' you are psychometrizing, and you can learn much from them. It is important never to get distracted from the task at hand – to give as powerful and effective a healing treatment as possible. Any impressions you receive should be used only within this context. You should not start off with a healing treatment and get diverted through the impressions you are getting into an uninvited psychic reading, or an opportunity to test your own accuracy!

Related to psychic touch is dowsing, either through divining rods or a pendulum. You would need specific training to perform either of these psychic skills, but if you do find that you are naturally responsive to psychic touch, you might decide to take up dowsing. The pendulum, in particular, can be a very useful device in healing work. It is a bobbin on the end of a cord which moves in a clockwise or anti-clockwise direction depending on the reading you are receiving. These bobbins can be made of many materials, but if you intend to use it with healing I would recommend wood, since crystals or metals can very often pick up and retain energies from the patient, whereas wood is not so radionically receptive to psychic energies. Some healers will judge, by the movement of the pendulum around the aura of a patient, where exactly healing is most needed. Even though the patient has told you what they are suffering from, the aura is so intricately interconnected with energies that healing may not always be required exclusively where a physical ailment is being experienced.

Smell

Psychic smell is something I have only experienced occasionally, but there are those who are able to glean precise information from it, especially in relation to health. The 'smell' of an illness can be unpleasant, and it would be understandable and practical if a healer decided to detach entirely from it so that they could better concentrate on the task at hand. However, it would be possible to develop this sense so that you could identify individual conditions from their smell.

Some subtlety is required in developing this ability, since the last thing you want to do is show a patient that you have sensed unpleasant smells around them! On the positive side, you could also become aware of the perfumed aromas of different healing energies, as you start to receive and transmit them.

Sight

Psychic vision, or clairvoyance, is the most commonly developed psychic ability – in fact, vision is the sense more people say they think in than any other. Memory, too, employs the sense of vision more than smell, taste, touch or hearing. Clairvoyance can be very useful in healing work, in that you will be able to see the aura and the colours in it, contaminated or otherwise. In performing the healing passes, if your clairvoyance is accurate enough you will be able to see where the contaminated energy needs to be scooped up. You will note the discolouration, which may not be in the exact areas where the patient feels physical pain, and work in these areas as well as in the location of the physical ailment, providing an extra charge of energy to balance it out. You will also register the free flow of healing energies entering the patient, and indeed yourself, beforehand, which can help you to become a better channel. It is inspiring to witness a flow of blue, green or purple energies entering the room in which you are working, rather like a stream of coloured air. This can make a major difference to your healing work, providing – and this is a vital proviso – you do not get carried away by the fascinating interplay of energies and thereby neglect the healing itself.

As with all other psychic attributes, you need to be wary of a vivid imagination getting the better of you, especially in the early stages. I would go so far as to say that all developing psychics make mistakes – they need to, in order to learn. However, you cannot afford to let such mistakes affect the treatment of your patient, so let your psychic development become a secondary consideration. If and when you become reliable as a psychic, you can start to take more notice of your impressions, but until then do not be ruled by them. Regard them as a kind of 'second opinion' to be acted on carefully and with discretion. I have met so many psychics who do not follow this advice, and who have ruined what could have been a most valuable skill by their over-exuberance and lack of discrimination. It is all a question of getting the balance right. It would be wrong to suppress your psychic potential, because if you don't use it, you'll lose it. It would also be wrong, however, to be ruled by it or dependent upon it.

Hearing

The beauty of psychic hearing, or clairaudience, is that as well as thoughts popping into your head as if from nowhere, so do sounds. These will probably take the form of an accent or intonation with the words, denoting that they come not from you but another communicator. I have to stress that a massive health warning goes with all this – psychopaths, as well as wise spiritual teachers, believe that they hear voices. I have met many spiritual people who've believed themselves in touch with higher beings, but who were really in touch with a lower one trying to confuse them – or with just their own imagination. It can be difficult to tell: sometimes it is indeed a higher being, and sometimes what you think is a higher being is coming from your own mind. I apologize for muddying the waters with all these possibilities, but there are enough irresponsible teachers out there already and I do not wish to add to them. Well-intentioned as most of them are, the road to hell is paved with good intentions.

So too is the road to heaven, and clairaudience can be a most wonderful way of gaining helpful guidance from those who have a deeper insight than we have into the healing process. A good rule of thumb to help you discriminate between genuine and false contacts is that a communicating intelligence will be at a similar level to the person they are communicating with. The clairaudient must be able to induce an equivalent level of consciousness, at least while the psychic contact is being made, to the communicator. The important thing, though, is the message, and how useful it is for your healing. True clairaudience – which does not and should not involve any form of trance – can help you to make the distinction between messages from within or outside yourself.

Guides and Guardians

Angels are all over the place nowadays. There are lengthy books – and little ones too, for that matter – full of them. I have lectured extensively on this subject, in traditional church settings, at new age festivals and for charitable organizations, and have broadcast about it all over the world on radio and television. Sometimes it seems that everyone is into angels in one way or another – whether via a pagan ritual, an orthodox ceremony or their favourite hit record. This openness towards angelic visitations has to be welcomed, although it has also led to a lot of mixed signals about what angels really are. From the angel Gabriel with robe and trumpet all the way through to a deceased hospital porter wearing a T-shirt and jeans, the descriptions vary immensely.

There are those who rule out the possibility that angels can be those who have died and passed to higher realms, which I consider to be a big mistake. The truth is that 'angel' is just a word like any other. The fact that it is all things to all people only goes to indicate its undying significance.

Whatever people believe them to be, there is no doubt that angels are often seen clairvoyantly around healers, helping to manipulate the energies flowing through them. My own view is that they are mostly what would have been termed 'spirit guides' at one time, and are now more frequently called guardian angels. These are people who have physically died, but still inhabit higher spheres of existence. They are attracted by the light of healers at work and come to assist. They may be guides associated personally with the healer in question, or they may be more interested in the work at hand rather than the people doing it. The latter type of guide can actually be more helpful. They should not interfere in any way, but only offer seen or unseen help to the healer. If you do become aware of this type of assistance, it can be an advantage to co-operate with them, but it is certainly not necessary to do so. A healer should never be dependent upon guides or guardians, but treat them rather as very good friends for whom you have a deep respect. They are not infallible, but they can certainly assist.

There are those who believe that the angelic help they are getting comes straight from God, the Virgin Mary or some other source associated with their religion. This is very often a result of their beliefs crystallizing in a form they understand. Sometimes people will actually be working with a spirit guide, but believe it is something far more advanced than this.

Some guides will tolerate this on the basis that they can still get some good healing work done, and allow the person to hold whatever views their belief structure determines. In Tibet there are stories of spiritual entities called *dakinis*, manifesting in shapes to suit the person concerned, in order to make contact.

By and large, angelic help in healing work will be performed by more advanced people on the other realms, who have not yet reincarnated in the physical world but who wish to help. Providing they do not exert any control over the healer or interfere with the healer's free will, which normally they won't, and providing their energy is helpful, which it is virtually bound to be, this is to be welcomed. They are not infallible; you should always stand on your own two feet and not rely on them, and I must stress that a healer who is aware of angelic help will not necessarily be more effective than one who is not. It is not something every healer needs to pursue, but for those who do – in a balanced, discriminating way – it can help and inspire.

Here are some verses to illustrate the concept of seeing angelic forces at work with healers.

Angelic Verses

They came,
In emerald green
And violet hue,
A landscape dream
Of gold and blue

Their thoughts shine down
Their words vibrate
To a mental sound
As the dreamer wakes
In reality

They saw,
The healing force
Kaleidoscope
From an infinite source,
An eternal hope,

The remedy,
A lasting cure,
Where love is free,
And so pure,
It conquers all.

It is unlikely that you will develop all the psychic attributes included in this chapter, nor is it necessary to do so. In fact, if it's a question of choice, it is far more important to have a realistic grasp of the practical requirements for becoming a healing practitioner.

7 Becoming a Practitioner

There is more to becoming a practising healer than administering a technique, even one as effective as the *King Technique*. The relationship you develop with your patient is crucial to the success of the overall treatment. And there are many pointers and principles you can and should follow to establish the right dynamics with your patient during a treatment.

Treatment Dynamics

To establish positive dynamics between patient and healer, it is necessary to build an appropriate relationship. This will vary from situation to situation, but there will be two main ingredients in this process: empathy and dialogue.

Empathy

The old-fashioned 'bedside manner' is described today as 'a positive
practitioner–patient relationship', but it amounts to pretty much the
same thing. The key ingredient is allowing the patient to express how
they feel about their condition. Empathy means demonstrating that you
understand where the patient is coming from, without being
judgemental.

Empathy can be divided into two categories. The first involves
demonstrating that you have understood what the patient has told you
about themselves, by repeating it back to them in one form or another.
The second comprises showing that you understand what is going on
under the surface of the patient's consciousness, which they either feel
unable to express or are not conscious of. By bringing these things out
into the open, whether they are constructive or not, you have shown
empathy with their situation. It is not just that you understand the
patient; it is that the patient knows that you understand.

The most valuable ability for establishing empathy is intuition. With
practice, you can know instinctively and immediately what is going on in
the patient's head and heart. You then have to show that you have
understood this, by expressing it back to them in a gentle, non-intrusive
way. This ties into the impressions you receive from your patient, as
outlined in Chapter 6.

Be careful how you express this knowledge: you should never be
dogmatic, or try to get the patient to reveal things they would rather keep
confidential. After all, they have come for a healing treatment, not a
session of psychotherapy, and they may just want you to get on with the
technique. In such a case you should not prolong the questioning,
though you still need to ascertain some information from them about
their condition. You will get other patients who just want to open up to
you, either before or after the treatment – it should never be during a

treatment, because this would dissipate the energy they should be receiving from you and taking within their aura. If they do want to open up to you, allow them to do so. Empathy does not mean that you have to agree with the patient's viewpoint; it just means that you understand how they feel, and this can provide crucial information about their condition.

Having understood their mental and emotional state, and shown them that you understand, what do you actually say to them about it? This will very much depend upon the type of relationship they want with you. Some may want your opinions; some just to receive healing from you; others will want to lean on you and look to you for advice and guidance; most will be somewhere in between. It will be for you to discover into which category each patient falls, but you cannot necessarily give them exactly what they want all the time. The patient who resists all advice may well be the one who needs it most; the 'leaning' type of patient may go from person to person seeking advice, but would probably be better off learning to stand on their own two feet. All patients, however, will need an element of dialogue, if only to understand how best to co-operate with the treatment they are receiving.

Dialogue

Very often people come to healers as a last resort. This is the wrong way round – healing should be the first resort. Whatever other method of medical assistance a person may be receiving, healing will complement it and aid in their recovery, though you must be clear from day one that you offer no guarantees. Healing should be available in all the hospitals of the world and at every doctor's surgery, and I believe that one day it will be. In the mean time, patients very often need to be educated in the principles of psychic and spiritual healing. It is really best described as natural healing, because nothing could be more natural than transmitting the universal life-forces through yourself and into another. The *King Technique* is one very precise and accurate way of doing this.

Most patients need to bring about change in their lives. Given that the majority of illnesses include emotional or psychological factors, by definition there is or has been a mental or emotional imbalance of some kind. Even if there is no pre-existing psychological element, an illness or injury will have some kind of effect upon a patient's emotional or mental make-up, especially if it is a serious condition. A determined outlook can make all the difference. How much you can steer the patient in a more positive direction will depend entirely upon the natural relationship which is being formed between you. There should be no attempt to talk down to or patronize the patient, or to inflict your pet theories of better living upon them uninvited. However, in most cases there will be a natural opportunity to pass on advice of one kind or another. The golden rule in creating dialogue with a patient is: Education with respect.

From the patient's point of view, they should feel a sense of gratitude for receiving healing, and part of the function of the dialogue process will be to encourage this – not for your sake but for theirs. One of the most positive states of mind you can experience is thankfulness and appreciation, whereas bitterness eats away at your mind and emotions in a highly destructive way. The patient's gratitude can be expressed both in their approach and through making some kind of financial offering. On the whole, I would not recommend healers to charge a fixed fee, through an increasing number do and, in one sense, they have every right to do so. They are providing a very valuable service, and they have to live. There can be no ethical objection whatsoever to a healer charging for their time, except that the healing itself does not come from them exactly, but from the universal supply, through them. Even so, if they need to charge in order to heal, they have every right to do so. If it is a voluntary activity rather than a professional one, which in most cases it is, I consider that the magic of healing is better and more powerful without a fixed charge. This does not mean that the patient should not give something – they should always be encouraged to donate within their means as a tangible expression of their appreciation. This can then be put towards further healing work or the expenses of running a healing practice, rather than used as direct income for the healer.

Patients who do not give anything, either financially, through co-operation with the healing treatment, or preferably both, will tend to be less fortunate in their recovery. They are trying to receive without being willing to give, and that flies in the face of their Karma, which requires them to sow in order to reap.

Although every ailment can be cured through healing, some patients are very difficult to cure because of their attitude. In a case like this, you will have to encourage them to stand on their own two feet by improving their diet, exercise and mental outlook, or whatever else comes out in your conversation with them. You may not be qualified to give specific advice in some areas, but you can advise them to consult someone who is. They need to make more effort towards their recuperation in one way or another – to put some energy into their health before it can improve.

People are increasingly aware of the professionalism of practitioners of all kinds, and have come to expect a first-rate service. Whether you are providing your healing as part of a professional therapy practice or on a purely voluntary basis, you should try to ensure that your treatments are as well organized and professional as possible. In Britain in the year 2000, complaints against medical doctors to the General Medical Council increased by 50 per cent, which shows two things. First, the public have higher expectations nowadays from medical practitioners and are willing to complain if they do not get them. Secondly, the orthodox medical doctor is no longer regarded as an unquestionable authority who knows all there is to know about medicine. People are turning more and more to complementary medicine as well, which is to be welcomed. I certainly do not wish to criticize in any way hard-working doctors who offer an invaluable service to their patients. Their treatment is not the be-all and end-all, but it should never be denigrated by healers. *Responsible healers will never recommend their patients to ignore medical advice; on the contrary, they will work with other forms of treatment in a constructive way to bring about the best possible results for the patient.*

Structuring a Session

As a practitioner, it is vital to organize the structure of your treatments correctly. For simplicity, I have divided this into five stages: welcoming, listening, explaining, treating, and guiding your patient.

Welcoming

The way you first meet your patient will set the tone for the whole treatment. It will vary from patient to patient, but essentially you need to put their mind at rest. Some patients will be very familiar with the principles of healing already; others will regard it as far-out, slightly risky even, but worth a try. You need to establish a combination of warmth and confidence from the start. Your warmth will make them feel comfortable, and your confidence in what you are doing will reassure those who are not sure what healing is all about. How much of each is necessary will depend upon the patient's psychology, not yours.

Your task when you first meet a patient is to exude an air of friendly, welcoming competence. How you do this will, again, vary according to your personality. If you are the type of person who is naturally humorous, you can use that to good effect; if you are naturally quiet and calm, then that will be just as effective in establishing a warm atmosphere. Use your own natural qualities to achieve a comfortable atmosphere – bad jokes will not do it any more than shy embarrassment. Use the positive attributes of your own personality, and project them from the beginning. If you are still not sure how, turn back to Chapter 4 for some pointers.

On a practical level, the arrangement of your practice will be crucial. It may be that you have a receptionist assisting you, in which case it will be their job to make the patient feel comfortable, but your first meeting with them will still be crucial.

Listening

The first thing to do, having welcomed the patient, is to find out exactly why they have come to see you. It is always best to keep some kind of record of your patients and their general progress through a number of treatments. It is sensible to recommend that they come for several treatments (in the case of severe illnesses, for at least six), in order to see if it is working for them. If they come week in and week out for months and report no change whatsoever, it might be a good idea for them to try another type of therapy.

For a chronic condition, a weekly treatment is about right – you want to allow time for the energies to bring about inner change. If the condition is acute, twice a week should suffice, unless it is an emergency, in which case give them healing every day if possible. If their illness is in any way contagious, you should not treat them but send them absent healing over a distance, as described in Chapter 8. There is no point being a martyr in this respect, and thereby limiting your ability to heal other patients.

Ideally you would design your own registration form or card on which you'd keep details of all your patients. These must be kept absolutely confidential, and only completed with the permission of the patient, who could feel intimidated by your wish to keep a record. Explain that it is purely so that you can monitor their progress and thereby ensure that they receive better healing treatments, but if they ask you not to, you will have to respect their wishes. You can, however, decide whether you wish to treat them under such circumstances. I know that sounds hard, but you are putting yourself out for them and the patient should co-operate with any reasonable request. They would have no choice in a doctor's surgery, and it shows a lack of respect for you as a practitioner if they will not extend you the same courtesy.

In most cases they will give you the information you need, which is the following:

- **name, address and phone number**

- **age, if they are willing to give it; otherwise your own approximation**

- **the nature and a brief history of their complaint**

- **where exactly they feel pain.**

This will suffice for your needs, which are not diagnostic in the strict sense, but will give you enough information to proceed. *In fact, you will have to be very careful not to give anything which could be interpreted at any stage as a medical diagnosis, because this may contravene the law in some parts of the world.*

It would be worth enquiring what other types of medical treatment they are receiving. You might be shocked to discover that someone with a critical or even potentially life-threatening condition has not even informed their doctor. There are some who might need surgery but who will not go to a hospital. You cannot force them to do so, but you should certainly give them cautious advice, both for their sake and to cover yourself. You will be surprised just how some patients – not most of them, thankfully – can turn on you and blame you later. They can claim that you promised to cure them and told them they needed no other help, when in fact you did nothing of the sort except respond to their request for healing. Keep notes of your advice, and if necessary, and if it is serious enough, get their written acknowledgement that you have advised them to seek other medical help. In most cases the latter will not be necessary; but you may want to recommend that a patient with back trouble visits an osteopath or chiropractor as well as yourself, or that a patient with a digestive disorder seeks dietary advice – and, if you do so, record it.

Often while you are in listening mode, the patient will open up and other issues will come out unsolicited. It could be an emotional or psychological problem that they feel able to talk to you about. You will have to be careful that you do not lose all your healing time just listening, but it can be helpful for them to open up to somebody, possibly for the first time, about what is on their mind. Sometimes this is the real reason they have come to you. You can also recommend some type of counselling, if you feel they need it. If you are not a professional counsellor, you will have to be careful that it does not become a counselling session, which you are not qualified to handle. But listening for a short while, especially on a patient's first visit, can only help.

In subsequent weeks, pull out your records, ascertain how they have been since you last saw them, and obtain any other information they want to share with you which may be relevant.

Explaining

You will need to describe exactly what healing is and how it works. If you are using the *King Technique* as recommended in this book, explain that you are basically working on the aura, where their illness is reflected and very often is even the root cause of their psychosomatic condition. When the aura is in harmony, so, sooner or later, must the physical body be as well. Briefly run through the different stages of the treatment, differentiating between charging the major psychic centres and treating the specific ailment, so that they know why you are not going straight to the point of their discomfort. By taking them through the procedure you will be following, you will help them to relax into it.

Some patients seem to think that healing should work instantaneously, and if it does not that there is something wrong with the healer. I call this the 'miracle syndrome', because it derives from a religious or faith-based approach to healing rather than regarding it as a natural process which may take time to work fully. Certainly you will get your immediate responses from some patients, but with others it may take several sessions before the results start to show. Make clear from the start that, just as they would not expect instantaneous results from other forms of treatment, particularly if their condition is severe, they should not expect it from this one.

Healing works in a natural way, so there will be occasions when the patient will need to expel disease from their system before they can get better, and in doing so they can actually feel worse before they get better. This is also true of other holistic and naturopathic systems of medicine sometimes. But generally they should feel at least a sense of inner peace and sometimes a mild improvement from the first or second session. And, just occasionally, you might get that instantaneous miracle!

Your patient may not have the faintest idea what you expect of them during a healing session. Not just how they should sit – which you should explain clearly – but also what they should be thinking about. Again, your advice will vary from patient to patient. If they are a firm believer in healing, possibly a practitioner themselves of a method of natural therapy, you can ask them to visualize white light surrounding them. This will harmonize with your visualization and thereby potentize the whole treatment. Ask them to regulate their breathing as evenly and deeply as possible, which will help the absorption of spiritual power into their aura during the charging, and enhance the cleansing process during the passes. In many cases you may decide not to ask for co-operation like this, because it could bring out some reservations, which could act as a barrier to treatment. If so, just ask them to try to feel as peaceful as possible and to relax into the treatment.

Treating

You are now ready to start the treatment, about which nothing further needs to be said, except that you must remain sensitive to the patient's reactions to what is happening. Preferably the session should be conducted in as much silence as possible, but if you become aware of inhibitions or resistance, you may need to open up a temporary dialogue. You will also need to be sure you are not inadvertently causing any type of discomfort. Some healers go to the other extreme and open up a line of conversation, much as a hairdresser might, which is not appropriate to the situation. I say this having lectured to 150 hair salon-owners one evening, who were, I must say, an extremely open-minded and responsive audience. They informed me that, next to a doctor, they have more physical contact with their clients than any other profession, and I am sure there is a therapeutic aspect to what they do. But, in a healing situation, the energy will be dissipated by too much chat during the treatment.

Guiding

After the treatment is the time for you to give any guidance or advice that you feel the patient requires. This should only be done with the patient's co-operation. They will not listen to you anyway if they do not choose to. They could feel that they have come for healing, not to be lectured to, and they may object to having your ideas thrust upon them. On the whole, though, most are open to some type of guidance before their next session. To do this, you will need to employ both empathy and dialogue. Remember, empathy is the ability to see the patient's world through their eyes, to put yourself in their shoes, to suspend your own frame of reference and enter theirs. You have to demonstrate that you are 'with' their feelings and experience, and that you understand and accept them. Things may emerge from the patient which they had not realized they had felt before, and you can help them to see what is really troubling them. In a nutshell, you are tuning in to them – empathy is really an intuitive skill.

Carl Jung was one of the first psychologists to give intuition its true place as a source of human knowledge, when he divided human experience into four categories: sensing through the body; feeling through the emotions; thinking ideas through the mind; becoming aware of impressions through the intuition. His theory has had a profound effect: various schools of therapy and counselling now include intuition in one form or another.

As well as empathy, you will need a good dose of down-to-earth common sense, which can be strangely lacking in many patients. This is where the dialogue comes in. The most valuable advice you can give them is to adopt a positive approach to life. This does not mean lying to themselves, or pretending they are well when they are not. But they can and should try visualizing themselves getting better; reaffirming to themselves mentally that they are going to get better. This will ignite their subconscious mind and fire up the process of recovery by sending constructive signals of improvement through their physical and psychic nervous systems.

They will probably need confidence to believe this really works, but urge them to try it. Even using the familiar autosuggestion, *'Every day in every way I am getting better and better and better'* 10 minutes a night before going to bed can work wonders if only they try it for a while. And they should make whatever effort they can to help their healing process, rather than delegating the responsibility to the healer alone.

What further guidance you give will very much depend on your areas of expertise. I do believe in practising what you preach, and you cannot really give advice on diet unless you are qualified to do so, and follow a good balanced diet yourself. Similarly with exercise: you need to set the example of some form of regular physical exercise before asking your patient to do so. Very often, the best advice comprises simple things, which the patient already knows but needs encouragement to do. Be careful of receiving confidential information beyond their physical health. In the unlikely event that they confess a crime to you, for example, you might be legally bound to report them to the authorities, because you have no protection under law. As in the listening stage, you may have to set boundaries for the guidance part of your session by suggesting they seek some form of professional counselling.

Setting up as a Practitioner

There are two ways to set up as a practitioner: to work in an existing practice, or to start your own. Of course, the first is far easier. Either way, you should acquaint yourself with your legal position in the country in which you are practising, and make sure that whatever insurance you might need is taken care of.

You will also need to consider the best way to set up your financial arrangements. In The Aetherius Society, we do not charge patients and no healer receives any payment personally for giving healing. We accept donations towards the upkeep of our healing centres around the world, which can be fairly costly, and advise patients to contribute something within their means. Some are very generous and give us at least as much as if we had set a treatment fee. If they do not give anything, we still give them healing.

If you are working as a healer at a therapy centre, you may have to set a reasonable charge for your services. This will vary from practice to practice and region to region. If you are setting up your own practice, there will be considerable expenses involved, and budgeting will be a key factor.

Many healers do not wish to go this far: they work from home in an informal way. If all the patients are people known to you, this is fine, but if you are starting to get members of the public or people referred to you whom you know nothing about, there are some precautions to be followed. First, there is security. If you are alone in the house, you need to be very careful whom you treat – if in doubt, do not let them in. This may sound uncharitable, and it is somewhat untrusting, but there is no point in running unnecessary risks. You will not be much good as a healer if something happens to you which puts you off healing for life.

If possible, use a part of your home which is not used for anything else. I realize that most of us do not have this luxury, but a small room set aside for healing would be ideal. If this is not possible, make sure that you thoroughly clean the area you have used afterwards, both psychically (with the White Light or Violet Flame) and physically. Set aside a stool or chair which is purely used for this purpose, and preferably use clothing (beneath your white coat) which you wear only for healing.

Outside visits to patients have to be treated with caution. If you do not know the patient, it is advisable not to be alone with them, for security reasons. Assuming that they are bed-ridden, which is why you are visiting them, they will probably have a carer with them anyway.

Some healers work in hospitals or other health centres. This will depend on the rules of the establishment and the wishes of the patient. I have done this myself, and it can be very effective indeed. If the patient is confined to bed, you will have to modify the technique you follow, probably basing it on the self-healing version of the *King Technique*.

One word of warning: as soon as word goes around that you are visiting, you are liable to get many other requests, and will have to be firm about how much time you have to spend.

You may get requests to give healing to animals, which can work very effectively indeed. Animals love healing and are often far more aware of it than humans. They know that when you lay your hands upon them to give them a stroke that there is energy passing between you and them, and they literally lap it up. Obviously you will have to adapt the *King Technique* to the animal in question, but the main principles are the charging of affected areas; the passes to remove contaminated energy; and the smoothing of the aura at the end. One healer friend of mine has specialized for years in using this technique on animals, with great effect. In one case she gave healing to a champion basset hound who was suffering from a serious nervous condition. Although physically a champion, his mental disposition stopped him from winning rosettes. After three treatments, the dog was so much better he competed in a show of 1,000 entrants and won the 'Best of Breed' prize! Here is a testimony from an animal healer:

Testimony from an Animal Healer

'A horse broke a bone in her lower leg whilst being exercised. The vet agreed to put the leg in plaster but thought the animal would have to be put down within 24 hours. I gave her healing after his visit and again the next day. The vet was amazed to find that the injured leg had not swollen. He gave the horse a 48-hour reprieve. I then gave her two more lots of healing.

'The vet returned and x-rayed the leg, which, to his astonishment, had healed. As he expected to put the horse down, her leg had been set slightly crooked so she was unable to jump again. Her owner was able to use her for riding and bred several beautiful foals from her.'

Incidentally, animals can also give excellent healing themselves. Sometimes a cat will sit directly on your solar plexus centre when it knows that you are depleted in energy, and literally charge you up. Dogs often exude healing energy, especially towards their owners. Legend has it that Saint Rock, the 14th-century monk and patron saint of healing the plague, was himself healed of the plague by a dog. I have been into hospitals with a charity called 'Pets As Therapy' (PAT), which takes animals to patients, and interviewed several patients who believe that they received tangible healing from the pets. Two of the best healers were a three-legged dog and a one-eyed cat! It was as though they understood and empathized with the patients better. The owner of the three-legged dog told me that it has two siblings who are in very good shape physically, but are not nearly as good with hospital patients, so she leaves them at home.

Plants, too, respond to healing energies, as a number of experiments have proved. By blessing your plants as well as watering and nurturing them in other ways, you will improve their growth and life span. Try sending them healing energy and see how they respond – you might be amazed just what a difference it can make.

You can, in fact, heal all life, wherever you find it in the world.

8 *Healing the World*

This is the shortest, yet potentially the most important chapter of this book. If everyone applied the principles of healing to the world as a whole, it would change today.

So much time and energy is wasted in the world of ideas, which could be applied to the world of experience. (Some would call the latter the world of reality, but that would open up yet another philosophical debate, which would take us back to ideas again!)

Healing is not restricted to any one physical location, even a healing practice. It is not restricted to Egypt, Tibet or any other mystical location – it is all-encompassing, completely unlimited. It transcends all barriers, including mental ones. It is as big as that, yet it is hardly used. It alone could transform politics, science and religion:

It would be more useful and constructive if much of the time spent debating in the political chambers of the world were instead spent radiating positive healing energy to the situation being discussed.

Scientists could apply the principles of psychic matter and energy to any number of their convoluted theories. Unfortunately, the very simplicity of healing might put some of them off, because they are trained to look for and expect complexity, but a few are already embracing it.

Religions could dispense with their man-made dogmatic barriers and unite on this fundamental, practical method which could be at the heart of their faith. In their different ways they could send out powerful, positive energies to remedy the sickness of the world, rather than performing some of the more introverted ritualistic practices they sometimes engage in at present.

Above all, what's at issue is feeling a sense of worldwide responsibility, rather than an exclusively domestic one.

Thinking Globally

A global perspective is the true mark of spirituality. It is easy to love one's family and friends, and of course one should. But as soon as you say that these things are more important than the suffering of thousands or millions of others, just because they mean more to you personally, you have lost the spiritual plot. I would go so far as to say that a revolution of consciousness among humanity in this one respect would bring in a new age immediately. It is this small, insular domestic vision, eclipsing appreciation and responsibility for the whole, which limits us as human beings.

From family to tribe, tribe to community, community to nation, nation to human race, human race to all life on Earth: this is the journey of expanding spiritual perspective that we all need to take. We need to break down barriers: just looking out for our own is really only an extension of selfishness. Yes, let's look out for our own, but let's also look out for others, too, especially when their need is the greater.

All the heroes and role models of history have had an effect on the world as a whole – whether it be at a cultural, scientific, political, philosophical or religious level. We all know that this is what really counts, yet too often we cling onto just making a difference in our own small circle.

One of the psychological reasons for this, I believe, is that many people do not realize they can contribute at a global level. They think they can make a difference to those they love, so that is what they will do, with a little charity added here and there. Just as great minds sometimes think alike, so too can limited ones. But this limitation can be cast off. Everyone can make a difference at a world level, through the power of healing. It can be sent anywhere you determine, be it a war zone or an area of natural disaster, and if world leaders won't make these responsibilities their first priority, then perhaps the healers of the world should.

So how do you send healing over a distance? Let's start with healing patients who are too sick or live too far away to be treated by you, or who have a contagious illness. You can still treat them – with Absent Healing.

Absent Healing Technique

Here again I will introduce the techniques of Dr George King, which give a definitive guide to the practice of healing over a distance. His words are in italics, with my commentary in ordinary type.

To send out Absent Healing, you as the healer must prepare yourself just as you would for a Contact Healing, with the same care, i.e. showering the body so that it is clean, putting on scrupulously clean clothes and your clean white Healing smock or coat, and then stand facing east and invoke the power within yourself. This is done by ... [performing the Practice of] the Presence ... doing some deep breathing ... and by Prayer. Go through this ritual in the order as given and you will soon be filled with natural Healing powers.

The ritual of preparation will become second nature to you after a while, so much so that immediately the energies will start to flow through you. On the face of it, it is not necessary to cleanse yourself physically and wear the white coat for healing over a distance, but it has become part of the magic of the technique. By making the same effort that you would for a healing treatment in your physical presence, the whole exercise will be more powerful. The Practice of the Presence and the breathing exercises will cleanse and charge you at a psychic level, as will the practice of prayer, if you are comfortable with this.

When you are so filled, put your arms outwards, with palms on the left and right hand side of you so that the action of the positive and negative psychic centres corresponding to the centre of each palm, is not in any way inhibited, with your fingers straight upwards and not bent, as in illustration [22].

This is the posture one imagines Jesus and his disciples adopted when they went to the hills to pray. It is far removed from the crouching position with hands clasped so often adopted in churches. This position, which is also the one to adopt for prayer, enables a free flow of spiritual energy from the psychic centres in the palms of the hands and the heart centre.

*Then you visualize a **white** light leaving the palms of your hands and – if you are able – your Heart Centre as well, and travelling **quickly** to the patient, charging them up from head to toe with this radiant Healing power; holding the visualization, at the same time, of their body and aura being fully charged with this power and them being in radiant health. If you know of any ills or deformities suffered by your patient, **do not recognize these** in the visualization as existing, but visualize your patient in perfect, radiant health.*

This technique can be adopted for a patient whether they are bedridden or not.

Illustration 22: Absent Healing Position

Your ability to focus your concentration exclusively on these visualizations will determine the success of this treatment. With practice, you will feel the flow of energy through yourself, either as warmth in the palms of your hands or as a tingling sensation around your body and aura. Even so, keep up the visualization of white light and try to feel a strong (but impersonal) love for the patient so that this love conditions the energy with a healing power.

It is very important that you do not imagine the illness that you know the patient has, because that would give power to it. Instead your focus should be on them as being in perfect health, and always surrounded by the white light you are sending them. This will act as a positive carrier wave of recuperative, strengthening energy. If the patient is bedridden, do not visualize them as such, but in full health.

It would be beneficial if the patient reciprocated by co-operating with you, therefore, you would have to make a prearranged time and stick strictly to it, so that the patient would know when you were sending the Healing ... All the patient has to do is to lie or sit quietly, facing East if possible, but not absolutely essential, and allow the Healing power to flow through them.

This will depend very much upon the individual patient. I would advise you always to get their permission before sending Absent Healing, so that they cannot object if they find out later. You would be surprised that some patients will even accuse you of harming them through your healing, because of their narrow-mindedness or because they are just looking for someone to blame. Such a patient would put up subconscious barriers against healing energy, anyway, and reject it when it was sent to them. However, their active co-operation is not absolutely essential. You can still send effective healing without it. But if you get full co-operation, this is better because they can allow the healing to bring maximum benefit by being in a receptive condition at the exact time that the healing is sent.

Another method which has been tried by groups of healers in The Aetherius Society and proved to be extremely effective is this. They get the patient to sit or lie quietly at a prearranged time, preferably at night, looking at a blue light in front of them. The patient is concentrating on this blue light when the Healing is sent. This is particularly effective because we have the concentration of the patient directed towards the blue light and, in some cases, this allows the Healing power to flow through them more easily.

The more effort the patient makes, the better it is for their recovery. A blue light can be purely a coloured bulb or an ordinary bulb with a blue shade over it. Some people use a slide projector with a 'Cinemoid' slide of pure blue, which is projected onto a screen. They then bathe in this coloured energy by sitting between the projector and the screen.

If you are treating a patient some distance away, possibly in another country, whom you have not met physically, then the usual procedure is to have a written report from this patient or a relative or another person representing this patient every month at least.

This is the least they can do, and you should not be willing to go on longer than a month sending regular healing unless they are willing to do this. In a severe case, you may want to give healing several times a week, but an ongoing chronic condition could receive a treatment weekly. It will depend on your schedule and the amount of patients you have, but it should be performed regularly, spending a few minutes on each patient before you move on to the next one. If you do not know them, you can ask for a photograph. Otherwise, use their name to enhance the psychic connection, which will have already been established through correspondence with them or their sponsor. You should maintain whatever patient–healer relationship you can; the general guidelines in Chapter 7 will apply in correspondence or phone contact as much as in person.

... if the patient has to go into hospital to undergo a surgical operation and you know the time of this operation, then you can make sure that you send

*them Absent Healing for a least 15 or 20 minutes **during the operation***
and also after the operation.

A good procedure to adopt is the following. Your patient has undergone a
medical examination. The doctors are not sure whether or not they have to
go into hospital until X-rays and other tests are made. The patient or
relative [or their sponsor] informs you of this over the phone or through the
mail. Immediately you tell them that you will send Absent Healing and
make a time so that they can concentrate in one of the ways outlined ...
you send the first Absent Healing treatment for 10 or 15 minutes. After a
few days, back come the reports of the test and the patient has to go for
another medical checkup and to hospital for surgery ... When they are in
hospital and you feel they have settled down, probably sometime during the
first evening, send another Absent Healing treatment of 10 to 15 minutes
... if the patient can tell you the exact time of the operation, it will be
extremely valuable. [When you have this, adopt this procedure:

> **approximately 30 minutes after the scheduled start of the**
> **operation,] send 15 minutes Absent Healing.**

> **[3 hours after the operation,] send another 15 minutes Absent**
> **Healing.**

> **[4 hours after that,] another 15 minutes Absent Healing.**

> **... if the operation has been extremely serious, try to send another**
> **15 minutes Absent Healing [3 hours later].**

... You will find with Absent Healing that a number of short treatments
are, in most cases, far more beneficial than one long treatment.

... Eventually your patient leaves hospital and is recuperating ... keep
sending the treatments in the morning, afternoon and evening ... [until
their convalescence is complete]

This procedure is obviously the ideal. The timings may or may not be convenient for you, depending on when the operation is taking place, so you will have to adapt it accordingly. Currently, operations are frequently delayed and, unless you have a direct line through to the hospital, you will have to judge the situation. If you follow this procedure, it can be very effective indeed.

Absent Healing can be performed alone, but it also works very well in groups. In this case a group leader reads out a list so that all the healers present are focused on the same patient at the same time. Here are a few examples.

- A woman from Spain had breast cancer and received intensive Absent Healing. After only a few months, she had recovered so much that she could go back to work, and was told that it was no longer necessary for her to have a mastectomy.

- A woman from New Zealand was scheduled to enter hospital for the removal of her entire large intestine. She underwent the arduous four-hour operation with little discomfort, and only 10 days later was discharged on a normal diet with no need for painkillers. The healing had worked in a perfectly complementary way to make the surgery far smoother and more painless than it would otherwise have been.

- A man from Hemel Hempstead suffered from acute leukaemia and a severe chest infection. He received regular healing from healers in different parts of Britain for several months, alongside orthodox medical treatment, after which he was completely cured and able to live a full and normal life.

- A man from Victoria, Canada had a serious head injury resulting in severe depression, leading to suicidal moods and an inability to work. After extensive Absent Healing, he recovered enough to work again and went through what his wife described as a positive transformation in himself, with much greater confidence and happiness.

- A woman from London suffered from fibrous dysplacia, a cancerous bone disease affecting her face and jaw. She received Absent Healing from around the country, alongside major surgery. Her surgeons told her that they were amazed by her speedy progress, and confirmed that the cancer would not return.

- A woman from Trinidad had three benign tumours on her brain. She received Absent Healing for three months, during which she also received successful surgery. Her recovery was so rapid after surgery that only a month later she was medically cleared to return to work, and felt absolutely fine.

Absent Healing is something that is adaptable to all situations. You cannot always follow exact rules, but have to respond to the situations of life. For example, you may come across an accident while driving, which is already being attended to by an ambulance or other qualified medics. Safely pull your car up further along the road, park and send a few minutes of Absent Healing both to the injured parties and those assisting them. This energy will help in such an emergency situation more than you might think. Here is a testimony from a patient who's life was changed by Absent Healing:

An Absent Healing Testimony

'After having had two heart arrests within 36 hours of each other, I understand that healers were asked for their prayers and absent healing. After 17 days in hospital, of which eight days were in the special coronary care unit, I have now returned home again (11 November 1999), ALIVE and well, although still fairly weak.

'Here is the result of all the healing sent to me. When visiting my doctor for a check-up he pronounced: "If I had not read your hospital report, I would not have suspected that you have had two complicated heart arrests."

'It is therefore with thanks to God that I would like to thank all those of you who prayed for and sent healing to me. Be assured that your absent healing worked miracles.'

Never underestimate your own efforts. You can become a channel for healing in all kinds of situations, not only for individuals but for groups, nations and the world as a whole. This is the true meaning of prayer.

Prayer

For many people, the word 'prayer' has unattractive connotations of religion and dogma, when really it is the most natural of human processes. Another term for it would be 'channelling energy', because that is really what it is. Prayer is a form of healing channelled according to a specific wording and/or visualization. Unfortunately, it has become tainted with selfishness. To put it bluntly, people tend to pray for themselves rather than others. It is something they do when they are in difficulties, as a final act of desperation. Even atheists frequently turn to prayer on the off-chance that it might help them out. Others use it as a kind of declaration of their faith, or some form of personal relationship they are conducting with a divine being. It can be all these things, but its real purpose is to send healing power through you and out to those whose need is greater. It is not restricted to health, but can be used to promote such world forces as inspiration, peace and freedom. A major claim, admittedly, but prayer can be a major power for good.

I received a report of a good example of this from a group of healers in Ghana. In May 1996, they had decided to devote a week to praying for peace in nearby Liberia, where a violent war was under way. After only the first day of prayer, 4,000 stranded Liberian refugees on a ship, which had been refused entry into several countries, was suddenly allowed to dock at Takoradi port in Ghana. Two days later, it was reported that the warlords who had started the war were requesting a cease-fire. By the end of the week, CNN reported that life was beginning to return to normal, and that only sporadic shooting between rival soldiers could be heard. Cash, donations, medicine, food and clothing from overseas were received by the Ghana government to help care for the refugees, and new talks were underway to restore peace. This looked like a result!

The next time you are watching a tragic news item on television, instead of feeling depressed and helpless, there is something that you, as a healer, can do about it.

Switch off the television and stand in the same posture you use for Absent Healing (see illustration 22), though not necessarily in a white coat. This is far better than kneeling with your head in your clasped hands, as so many do, thereby severely restricting the free flow of spiritual energy out to the world. Say a little prayer of request to God, Brahma, Allah, Jehovah, the Universal Spirit or whatever name you are most comfortable with, asking to be used as a channel for spiritual power to flow through you to the situation in question. Try to keep your visualization as positive as possible, just as you do in Absent Healing. Instead of visualizing the region as you saw it on television, which might be war-torn or disease-ridden, see it as bathed in white light, harmonized and healed. Do not try to influence specific politicians or other people involved to change their minds or their views, because that is an attempt to control them; it is not the correct magic of healing, no matter how much you may believe you are right. Just send them light and love by visualizing white light flowing through you out to this region, and visualizing it at peace, full of freedom and healed from suffering.

You might think that one person is insignificant in such a major problem. I beg to differ. The world is constantly being changed by people's thought patterns, be they good or bad. We have created the sea of mind energy that we live in, and the result is the world we have: material wealth and appalling poverty; good health and tragic sickness; desperate conflicts which go back thousands of years; heroic charitable work in desolate regions; a hotchpotch of values, philosophies and ways of life. All the thoughts of all the people in these situations are creating the results we witness every day. By sending out positive spiritual thoughts tempered with heartfelt love through the power of prayer, you will make a difference.

This is the great, transmuting energy, which will inspire and heal people throughout the world. The difference is that you will never know what good you have done, whereas in Absent Healing you will receive a regular report about your patient. But, you could save a life the night you switch the television off and say that prayer from your very soul. And that makes it worth a try, and another, and another ...

9 Living the Magic

You have now learned everything you need to become an effective and successful healer. I cannot think of a more worthwhile thing to do with your life than dedicate it to healing, and there is certainly nothing the world needs more than healing energy. From this will flow all the other forms of more material well-being that are needed. After all, there is not a shortage of money or food in the world as a whole; there is just an unwillingness to share it.

There is no need at all for warfare, except as a result of people's mindsets. If these changed, then war would be seen for what it is – an insane anachronism. Like human sacrifice, it would be seen as a primitive aberration which should be immediately dispensed with.

It all comes back to consciousness, and the only thing that can change this is the right kind of energy. Healing power can do it; it is as big and important as that. Many do not wish to take it that far. They want to learn healing as another skill to use from time to time, perhaps in conjunction with other therapies. For those of you who relate to that, this chapter may be superfluous. But others of you will make healing an integral part of your life; it will virtually become your path. And, believe me, as someone who has tried and tested this path for 30 years, it works in a way which can only be described as magical. It really does change your life completely.

So, for those of you who want to take this magic even further into your lives, I have come up with eight key aspects which, in keeping with traditional magic, I have called *rites*. So, if you want to live the magic, go ahead and read your rites!

Rite One: Gaining by Giving up Gain

This is the great paradox. Just as those who seek enlightenment only start to become enlightened when they realize that they are not, so those who seek complete life fulfilment have, at some stage, to give it up for others. Why is it that those who work for years and years to become famous find that when they do achieve fame, it does not hit the spot? Or that those who dedicate their lives to becoming rich are never totally satisfied, because someone else is always richer or more powerful than they are? Because the only thing that brings lasting satisfaction is what you do for others. When you look back on your life, it is not the size of your bank balance at particular times that gives you a deep glow within; nor is it the power you wielded over others. It is what you did in your relationships with others: for your children; for other members of your family and friends; for animals; for the local community; what mark you made upon people in general; what you did for the world; and especially what you leave behind you that would not have been left without you and others like you. These are things that really count in your innermost feelings.

We are enslaved by our needs. Those who seek power for its own sake, whether at work or in politics, are always insecure. They do not trust the motives of those around them. To take an extreme example, Stalin wielded unprecedented power in the massive Soviet bloc, and yet was so insecure about assassination attempts by his own colleagues that he spent much of the time locked away so that nobody could get to him. He was a prisoner of the very power he had sought. To take a more familiar example, how many people who tell their partner they love them actually mean they *need* them? When you eliminate need, you become free to love.

Someone living in a modest environment, who is at peace with that very modesty, is free. A richer person who craves more than they have is enslaved by that craving, they are not free. A person who lives alone often receives the pity of those who have a large circle of family and friends and constant companionship on tap. This pity is based on the assumption that the person who lives alone is lonely, when in fact they might be far less lonely than the person who cannot be alone. That inability to enjoy your own company enslaves you to the constant need for companionship, and when you do suddenly find yourself alone, you cannot abide it.

If you are able to satisfy your needs in life – and we all have them in one way or another – then you will lead a fulfilled life. The most effective way to do this is to concentrate on what you do for others. By sacrificing your own personal gain, you will actually gain the most valuable thing of all: freedom from need.

You can test this easily. When you next feel down or depressed by something that is going on in your life, look at the world as a whole and the problems in it. Your own problems will evaporate. I recently met a well-known television personality who told me he had absolutely no problems in his life, was fully content and therefore had no need of any form of self-help. He was a very pleasant person to meet, and I have no reason to doubt his sincerity. However, one thing I did point out to him was that anyone who is fully content in this world all the time must be a selfish person. Even if you have no problems whatsoever in life, which would be unusual to say the least, there are plenty of other problems in the world, which should surely cause some concern to you. How can you be happy and content when you hear about a major disaster or the personal tragedies which some people endure? Only by being completely self-absorbed, in which case, sooner or later, your life will change – and it will be all the harder because you are so used to being content!

By becoming engaged in the problems of others, on the other hand, you give yourself the best protection against this type of change, because you are not dependent on your life staying the same for your satisfaction. You have eliminated this need.

Rite Two: The Philosophy of Feeling

Healing cannot be a cold, intellectual thing – it is all about feeling. You start to develop a healing persona wherever you go. It is not just something you do, it becomes your whole philosophy. This does not mean a subservient personality – always being nice and easy – far from it. One of the shocks of my life has been to discover just how often it is necessary not to be nice. I have learned the hard way that you can be too trusting, not just from your point of view, but from the point of view of the person you are putting your trust in, as well. Instead of blossoming, they can sometimes take more than is good for them.

When you look at the planet as a whole, this is hardly surprising. The world needs some unpleasant truths and sharp lessons, as well as understanding and compassion. In fact, these lessons and truths could be the measure of that very compassion. A saint is not someone who never raises their voice in disagreement – or, if so, the world does not need such saints. The world needs patience and calmness, but also a very definite wake-up call.

The difference is that the healer will do this from a place of love. If you really care about someone, you will not always agree with them. It might be easier for you to agree; more comfortable to avoid confrontation. But it may not be the best thing. I was asked once by a magazine to write a column for them, on condition that I never at any time disturbed or upset any of their readers. Regrettably, I had to decline! If I had never disturbed or upset anyone, it would have been a useless column. We do not need writers to reinforce the mindset of the planet – we already have an advertising industry for that.

Upsetting people for the sake of it is just plain destructive, but we all need the occasional rebuke, delivered with the right, positive feeling. For this, look to the great spiritual teachers of history. Religions tend to focus on the attributes they are most comfortable with in their figureheads: forgiveness, tolerance, kindness and gentleness. We all want to be forgiven and tolerated in a kind, gentle manner – and there is an important place for that. But there is far more to Jesus, Buddha, Moses, Mohammed and Sri Krishna – just to name five spiritual leaders – than these qualities. They were all capable of being firm, disturbing, strict and, in certain instances, downright annoyed. If they had not cared, of course they would never have got upset with those they were trying to help, because they would not have considered them worth troubling about. But they came from a place of love.

The healer starts to vibrate to this energy of love, not just when giving healing but throughout life. They may not need a long, philosophical text to understand the meaning of life, but will feel and experience it as a living thing. Their priorities change – things which at one time seemed of crucial importance start to look petty by comparison with the big picture. The healer becomes less attached to personal emotions and more aware of love as a universal energy.

This does not mean that you lose your personal emotions as a healer – on the contrary, you will probably feel them more deeply than ever before. You will become more sensitive to the nuances of relationships and your interaction with everyone you meet. But you develop alongside this a greater ability to detach, and because of this you are capable of a deeper love than ever before. You are able to take it further because you have more control over it. And this feeling for others will extend to people you may never have even considered before, and to animals, plants, even your house and car. Everything lives and everything responds to feeling.

Rite Three: Everyday ESP

As your psychic powers increasingly start to inform your healing work, so they will extend into your everyday life if you allow them to. Because you are following a precise and disciplined technique, you will be able to switch them on and off, and you should always keep that ability. Healers who have learned another type of psychic healing have come to me because they have not been able to control the energies and experiences going on all the time whether they wanted them to or not. This will not happen to you if you follow the guidelines in this book. If you do start to find you are picking things up when you least want to, make a point of detaching; the subconscious mind will respond to a signal that you are not willing to enter a psychic state of consciousness at that time. On the other hand, extrasensory perception is a natural ability, and it would be a shame to turn away from it when it can help you and others so much.

We are conditioned to make all decisions solely through the faculty of reason. Everyday ESP means making decisions by what your gut feeling tells you as well. It does not mean that you should be constantly giving some type of clairvoyant reading wherever you go; that would be debilitating for you and irritating for everyone else. It means that you go by your impressions as well as what your logic tells you. If you buy a house, for example, conduct all the usual surveys and legal investigations, but also take note of what your intuition tells you. If you meet someone for the first time and have to make a social or work-orientated arrangement with them, take note of your first impressions about them. Do not be ruled by these impressions, but take them into consideration. Intuition can prove more accurate than reason in the long run.

As a healer you will become more and more sensitive to the vibrations from the people around you. This can become a telepathic skill, which should never be used in an intrusive way but can be very valuable. So often people do not say what they really think or feel. This can stem from inhibition, fear, excessive politeness or even because they have not come to terms with what they really think. An innate ability to know intuitively where people are coming from can help enormously in all aspects of life. It can also save you endless time, as often what people say hides, rather than reveals, their true feelings.

Sometimes your ability will develop further than this – you will pick up specific thoughts, possibly from people who are not even with you but desperately need you. You call them up and find that your telepathy is bang on. They had been unable to phone you themselves for one reason or another, but had really needed help at just that time. You had picked up a telepathic cry for help from them through the ethers of space.

As a regular broadcaster on radio phone-ins, I have received numerous reports from people from all walks so life about incidents in their daily lives where ESP has saved the day in one way or another. I remember a woman who told me she had a gut feeling one night to go and visit her parents. Everything rational pointed against it: she had a bad cold, the weather outside was severe, she might pass the illness on to her parents, so why not wait until tomorrow? But her gut instinct said, 'Go now.' Her parents did not have a phone, so she could not contact them that way. She followed her intuition and went round to their home – and that was the night her father died. She had received no warning of this likelihood, she just knew inside that she should go, and because she acted on her ESP she was there to say goodbye to her father when he passed away.

One specific extrasensory ability that you can gain is a sense of timing. So often it is not a matter of what you do, but when you do it. Hannah acted at the right time, despite all logic to the contrary. She did not know why, but she just knew she had to do it then. You may have had this type of impression before, but have you followed it? Did reason kick in and say, 'Don't be so silly,' 'That's not practical,' etc? You can make ESP a living force in your life. Don't be ruled by it, because we can all get it wrong, but don't ignore it either. It is a force to be reckoned with, listened to and acted upon.

Rite Four: Getting the Message

If you are able to receive guidance from higher beings when giving healing, this may extend at times into other aspects of your life. How much assistance you get will depend very much on what you are striving to do in your life. If your life is devoted to the upliftment of others, to inspiring people through some form of artistic expression, humanitarian project or spiritual activity, you are more likely to attract help from above. Angelic forces are not so interested in mundane materialistic pursuits, which they have cast off with the change they've been through called death. Certainly you may have guides who are concerned with you as an individual and watch over you, but they will only come to you from time to time when you need them, and generally when you are open to their help, which most people are not. In fact, one of the most frustrating tasks must be to guide the average person who does not believe in such things. There they are, trying to help people who do not even believe they are there, never mind listening to their guidance! Understandably, they frequently stay at arm's length.

If you start to live the healing path and allow it to permeate your whole life, however, you will attract another, probably more advanced level of guide or guardian angel who will be interested, not so much in your personal, day-to-day life (except where it impinges on your spiritual work) – they will want to help you to make a difference in the world. These can become your firmest friends and helpers, whether you know they are there or not. *I must stress again that those who are aware of and directly in contact with their guides are not necessarily more spiritually advanced or active than those who are not.*

Many people are rightly too occupied serving their fellow human beings through healing and other forms of service to devote attention to developing themselves in this direction. Such contacts are not for everyone, nor should they be. But for those who do go in that direction, here are some useful guidelines (sorry about the pun).

You should not become dependent upon them, or follow blindly wherever they lead – and if they are truly from a higher source, they will not let you. They will not want to control you, only to help you in your worthwhile task. There are so few people on this planet who dedicate themselves to genuine spiritual work that guides of this kind will literally be queueing up to help. They have been here and have learned that there is far more to life than they'd realized. They want to make up for this by helping those who are here to act differently, to seize the opportunities which they no longer have.

This is not the place for a full explanation of life after death – that is another book – save to say that, unlike this physical world, guides live with others of like mind. Here in the physical world we are all thrown together, good, bad and indifferent. Extreme wickedness stands side by side with the purest love. Gandhi was alive in the same period as Hitler, Jesus as Caligula, and in between such extremes a mass of differing peoples with varying aspirations. It is this physical world which needs to change, and the guides know this far more surely than they did when they were alive here. So they will grasp the opportunity to assist someone who is really trying to help the situation in positive, constructive, spiritual ways like healing.

If you become aware of this help, you may start to receive specific guidance in the form of a message. This can come as a thought, but not from inside your head – you will feel it entering from the outside. If you are clairaudient, you will actually hear it, not as a physical sound but as though it was a very real, strong voice from within. Here again, though, I have to give a massive health warning: Do not get carried away; often you will not know whether it's really your imagination or a genuine message from a guide. But with practice you can start to distinguish the difference by the state of consciousness you are in at the time. There is a difference between being in a receptive state, in which you receive a message from an outside source, and being in an inspired but active state of mind, in which case the thought may come from your own superconscious mind.

If you are able to go in this direction – and not everyone can or is meant to – then it can help you to live your life far more effectively, providing you keep your powers of discrimination at all times, analyse the messages you receive, and consider carefully if and how to apply them in your life.

Rite Five: Making it Happen

Everything that happens started somewhere, sometime as a thought. You become a healer because at some stage you are prompted or inspired to. The same applies to every other aspect of life. People sort out difficulties in their relationships because they both decide to do so. If only one of them makes this decision, it cannot work. All forms of success are achieved because the people who succeeded decided to. Those who had childhood dreams of achieving a particular career were visualizing it happening. Although this alone does not guarantee success, it is the beginning of it. As a healer you have decided to help people to get better, and because you are using a spiritual technique, the healing will be more permanent than is achieved by some orthodox therapies. This spirit of determination can spread to other areas of life as well.

If you have a problem area in your life – something you need to change – you can use the magic of visualization. If you are determined to achieve a particular goal, visualization can help make it happen.

There are just two provisos: First, your goal must be a worthwhile one, which fits with your destiny and capability. For example, there is no point in someone not suited to the legal profession setting out to become a lawyer. Or someone who is tone deaf using visualization to become a professional singer. You need self-honesty to establish your goal correctly. If it is the area of human relationships, for example, you may need to visualize yourself changing how you deal with others. Perhaps you are too aggressive, or perhaps too retiring. Visualize yourself changing, but not your whole personality being transformed. As a healer who uses visualization in your healing work, you will find it easier to perform such visualizations.

Secondly, never visualize other people changing against their will, because that would be a misuse of magic and would rebound upon you.

If you follow these ground rules, you can start to visualize any area of your life you wish to improve or change, manifesting as you determine it. Then leave it to destiny to determine the outcome. Just as you detach at the end of a healing treatment, detach at the end of your visualization and leave it to Karma.

Rite Six: Instant and Distant Karma

Karma is sadly misunderstood, by some, as a force which is out to get you. It has become for some a kind of spiritual paranoia – what will I get for doing this? In fact, Karma is a benign force which is out to help you. Even so-called 'bad Karma' is designed to give you the experiences you need to move forward, never as a punishment for this life or any other. Too often when people say 'I'm going to get some Karma for this,' they mean something negative is going to happen. This should be turned around completely; people should set out to create good Karma, both for themselves and for others. You cannot do one without the other anyway.

Just how instant Karma really is, is disputed. Traditional Hindus and Buddhists, who see Karma only as something you are creating for your next life, and who believe that everything that happens in this life is just a result of former ones, are missing the point. Your karmic pattern is moulded 24 hours a day, when you are awake and when you are asleep. Every thought and feeling has an impact upon it, as does everything you do and the full ramifications of how your deeds affect life around you. Irony apart, the idea of regarding Karma as instant brings a healthy change to the orthodox approach. It makes it a more real, living thing that can be monitored and adjusted on an ongoing basis, which is completely true.

However, it would be foolish to ignore that some of the things that happen can only be explained in conjunction with reincarnation, and it is positive to have the confidence that even if karmic benefits are not instantaneous, they will come in the future – even if it be a future life.

When you start to give healing, you will manipulate your own karmic pattern in a very positive and definite way. Because you are putting out healing energies, what goes around comes around. Positive energies will be returned to you in the form that you need them. You will start to advance spiritually, becoming stronger and more focused on the real priorities of life. You will start to be freer from a sense of loss and need – not because your expectations become lower, but because you will find satisfaction within. This may or may not be instantaneous. Sometimes people who take to the healing path find they are tested in the early stages, because a part of them is trying to resist this positive spiritual change. By remaining steadfast, you will get through and beyond this phase, should you experience it.

Life is not meant to be easy all the time; if it were, it would not be worth much because nothing would be learned or achieved. But, by and large, you will become more content and your health will certainly be better than it would have been if you were not a healer. As well as the short-term benefits, you will be shaping your long-term destiny and speeding up your evolution in this and future lives.

Rite Seven: In Tune with this Millennium

Times have changed, and healing is absolutely in tune with that change. If a person is suffering, some Hindu pundits would argue that it is their Karma and should not be interfered with. That is to miss the point entirely. You, the healer, can become the karmic instrument to change their pattern of suffering – it is, after all, part of the sufferer's Karma that they come to you as well.

This is the age of many things, but it is certainly the age of Karma. Another word for it is service. Nothing is more necessary, more fulfilling or more powerful a method of personal development than service to others. It works on every level. It is, I believe, the path for this millennium.

This is a time when artificial barriers are breaking down between peoples of all backgrounds. It is no longer possible to pursue one's own enlightenment without consideration for the world at large. Even if you were to find it, the great realization that would fill you would be that we are all interrelated with one another. There is no greater way to enhance your own evolution than to strive for the evolution of others. This type of approach becomes a positive spiral of experience which builds from itself. It is self-propagating, whereas a self-centred pursuit, even of spiritual awareness, does the opposite. It closes you off from the whole, and thereby diminishes your possibilities for karmic growth. In the massive and expanding self-help industry, this point is often missed. As a result, people can become more self-obsessed and need more and more seminars to get better, which of course is fine for the self-help business.

I am not denigrating self-help publications and workshops – I produce them myself – but they are not complete unless they make reference to service to others. Otherwise they will not teach their students the all-important element of how to improve their karmic patterns as well as their mental and emotion outlook. If the Karma is not right, then nothing else will work fully. I have found that a workshop which includes an element of healing or assistance to others will be far more effective at a purely self-help level – never mind the benefits it brings – than one which does not. You cannot, after all, breathe in without ever breathing out.

Healing is a perfect way of becoming more attuned to higher spiritual and psychic influences, and of releasing one's own psychic frustrations – which you may or may not be consciously aware of – as well as producing a positive karmic pattern for the healer. And these are only subsidiary benefits, because the main motive must always be to heal the patient, not to advance oneself. It is just that the two are interwoven – and service is always the first among equals.

Rite Eight: The Path of the Healer

There is much talk of what the new age really is. Some would say there is no such thing; others know better. It is the age of science and freedom and of individuality merged into the common good. It is also the age when so-called ordinary people can become outstanding people, not because of what they say or think, but because of what they do. Metaphysical thinkers have always been in danger of inhabiting the world of ideas, of being theorists. If life is the most serious of games, as some philosophers have said, then healers are among its most effective players. And their secret is that they are not playing to win, but to make it a better game for everyone else to play.

I have met literally hundreds of healers, using various techniques, in the last 25 years. Some honestly and openly admit that they have not got a clue why it works; they just know it is what they have to do, and they get on and heal people. Others I have come across have spent years trying to prove scientifically that healing works, and yet have never given a treatment. In 2000, the University of Maryland, after reviewing dozens of studies of prayer and healing, concluded that those who are prayed for do better than those who are not. Nevertheless, the findings were not regarded by academics as conclusive. In the mean time, those people who are being healed regard this evidence as quite conclusive enough. A lot of time can be wasted trying to convince others, instead of getting engaged in the practical business of healing people. Eventually the penny will drop and the medical establishment will open its doors even wider to healers, but I for one am not willing to wait until they do.

The true healer does not worry about belief or disbelief, appreciation or lack of it, or even results, though they are always welcome. He or she just gets on with the job, with heart, soul and, equally importantly, practicality. I had the opportunity to learn this balanced approach from working with Dr George King over many years. He could go from an elevated spiritual condition, in which healing was sent to thousands of people, to a thoroughly down-to-earth matter such as repairing a property to use for healing and prayer, or drafting a newsletter inviting people to take part. It is all part of the same project, just as the practical arrangements you have to make to give healing are as essential as the treatment itself. You have to be grounded in the here and now before you can aspire to the higher ground – if you were not, you would not be able to perceive it as being higher!

One of the great things about healing is that every type of person can do it. I have had the privilege of teaching the *King Technique* to hundreds of 'ordinary' people in New Zealand, Australia, the US, Nigeria, Belgium and Switzerland as well as Britain. These have included those from a Christian, Jewish, Buddhist, Hindu, Moslem, New Age, non-religious and multi-faith background. It really does not matter, as long as they give healing afterwards. I admire healers who get on and do it, so here's my poem for you all.

To The Healers

Sending out their energies,
Like concentrated melodies,
Of light-empowering remedies,
Reaching all extremities,
Some receiving messages,
And knowing how and when it is
The time to bless their enemies,
With heartfelt warmth and friendliness,
Which raises up their tendencies,
To new and powerful frequencies
Of love.

Becoming a healer is a wonderful calling. You can change and even save people's lives. At the very least, you will bring comfort to them. It will inspire and uplift you; it will also sadden and frustrate you at times. You will become more intuitive, and probably more psychic. You will start to radiate energy naturally, and become a more dynamic personality. You will be on a path of real service, and there is nothing greater than that.

There will come a time when this kind of healing will be the norm, when people will find it strange if there is not a psychic or spiritual healer on hand in every medical practice. Until then, it remains a pioneering activity. I could say that if you decide to become a healer, 'You won't regret it,' 'You know it makes sense,' 'What have you got to lose?' or even 'Give it a try!' But these sound too much like platitudes, so I won't – even though they're all true!

Appendix

The *King Technique* is performed regularly by healing practitioners in many countries of the world, including Great Britain, the United States, Australia, New Zealand, Canada, Nigeria, Ghana, South Africa and many others. Training workshops are run by The Aetherius Society specifically for those who have purchased this book, enabling you to test your skills and qualify as a healer in your own right. Guidance is also available from the Society on how to give and receive Absent Healing and Self-healing.

For further information, please contact one of the following addresses, which will put you in touch with your nearest Aetherius Society Healing Centre:

European Headquarters
The Aetherius Society
757 Fulham Road
London SW6 5UU
Tel: 020 7736 4187
e-mail: healing@innerpotential.org

American Headquarters
The Aetherius Society
6202 Afton Place
Hollywood, CA 90028
Tel: 323 465 9652
e-mail: healing@aetherius.org

Reference Notes

Chapter 1

1   Schwartz is a graduate of Harvard and was a professor at Yale before moving to the University of Arizona as a professor of psychology, medicine, neurology and psychiatry.

2   Russek worked with Schwartz as clinical assistant professor of medicine at Arizona University.

3   This is an extract from the journal *Scientific American*, published in 1979.

4   Dr Parnia was a clinical research fellow and Dr Fenwick a consultant neuropsychiatrist, both working at Southampton General Hospital.

5   Benjamin Libet was a neurophysiologist and Bertram Feinstein a neurosurgeon working at Mount Zion Hospital in San Francisco in the 1970s.

Chapter 2

1   Dr Maggie Price worked at the University of Iowa and Dr Gary
    Lewin at the Max Delbruck Centre for Molecular Medicine in
    Berlin.

2   Emiliano Macaluso worked with Professor Chris Firth and
    Professor Jon Driver at University College, London on this
    research.

Chapter 4

1   Dr George King used a deep samadhic trance to act as a medium
    for the Master Jesus in 1958 for a series of teachings called *The
    Twelve Blessings*.

2   Professor Charles Figley was in the psychology department of
    Florida State University.

3   This statistic was published in 1994 in a report from the Audit
    Commission in Great Britain.

4   Professor Martin Seligman was based at the University of
    Pennsylvania Psychology Department.

5   Paul Martin was a Fellow of Wolfson College, Oxford.

6   Howard Brody was based at Michigan State University.

7   Professor Herbert Benson was based at the Mind/Body Medical
    Institute at Harvard University.

Bibliography

Capra, Fritjof. *The Tao of Physics* (Flamingo, 1983)

Goswami, Amit. *The Self-Aware Universe* (Tarcher/Putnam, 1995)

King, George. *The Nine Freedoms* (Aetherius Press, 1963)

—, *The Twelve Blessings* (Aetherius Press, 1958)

—, *You Too Can Heal* (Aetherius Press, 1976)

Leadbeater, C. W. *The Chakras* (Theosophical Publishing House, 1927)

Peat, F. David. *Synchronicity* (Bantam, 1987)

Ramacharaka, Yogi. *The Science of Psychic Healing* (L. N. Fowler & Co. Ltd., 1918)

Schwartz, Gary E. R. and Russek, Linda G. S. *The Living Energy Universe* (Hampton Roads, 1999)

Wilhelm, Richard. *I Ching (Book of Changes)* (Routledge & Kegan Paul Ltd., 1951)

Zukav, Gary. *The Dancing Wu Li Masters* (Bantam, 1979)

Index